First World War
and Army of Occupation
War Diary
France, Belgium and Germany

59 DIVISION
178 Infantry Brigade
Royal Scots Fusiliers
11th Battalion
8 May 1918 - 26 July 1919

WO95/3025/9

The Naval & Military Press Ltd
www.nmarchive.com
Published in association with The National Archives

Published by

The Naval & Military Press Ltd

Unit 10 Ridgewood Industrial Park,

Uckfield, East Sussex,

TN22 5QE England

Tel: +44 (0) 1825 749494

www.naval-military-press.com

www.nmarchive.com

This diary has been reprinted in facsimile from the original. Any imperfections are inevitably reproduced and the quality may fall short of modern type and cartographic standards.

© Crown Copyright
Images reproduced by permission of The National Archives, London, England, 2015.

Contents

Document type	Place/Title	Date From	Date To
Heading	WO 3025 59th Div 178 Inf Bde 11th Bn Royal Scots Fus 1918 May-1919 July		
Heading	59th Division 178th Infy Bde 11th Bn Royal Scots Fus. May 1918-July 1919		
War Diary		08/05/1918	30/05/1918
Heading	War Diary Of 11th G.G. Bn. Royal Scots Fusiliers From. 1st June 1918 To 30th June 1918.		
Miscellaneous	Herewith Copy Of War Diary For Month Of June, 1918.		
War Diary	Auchel	01/06/1918	17/06/1918
War Diary	Lisbourg	18/06/1918	30/06/1918
Heading	War Diary Of 11th Bn. R. Scots Fusiliers From 1st July 1918 To 31st July 1918.		
War Diary	Lisbourg (Sheet 44C).	01/07/1918	04/07/1918
War Diary	Delette.	05/07/1918	05/07/1918
War Diary	Lisbourg	07/07/1918	23/07/1918
War Diary	Barly (Lens 11 G3/60.)	24/07/1918	31/07/1918
Heading	War Diary Of 11th Royal Scots Fusiliers. For August 1918.		
War Diary	Barly (51C P15.)	01/08/1918	02/08/1918
War Diary	Brickfield Strong P1. 51B/S2.3	03/08/1918	17/08/1918
War Diary	Barley 51C P 15.	18/08/1918	24/08/1918
War Diary	Ham En Artois 36 A.O.	24/08/1918	27/08/1918
War Diary	St. Venant 36A P.q.c vd.	28/08/1918	31/08/1918
Heading	War Diary Of 11th Royal Scots Fusiliers September 1918.		
War Diary	36A/Q 11 B 7.1	01/09/1918	08/09/1918
War Diary	Trenches Fauquasart. 36/M18.	09/09/1918	10/09/1918
War Diary	Corps Main Defence Line (Purple)	11/09/1918	12/09/1918
War Diary	Corps Res Defence Line (Red Dotted) 36A/R18C 32	12/09/1918	20/09/1918
War Diary	Bout Deville	12/09/1918	21/09/1918
War Diary	M17E 5.5	22/09/1918	23/09/1918
War Diary	La Bassee Rd M14d 9595 (near Ponr Du Hem)	27/09/1918	29/09/1918
War Diary	M17C 5.5	29/09/1918	30/09/1918
Heading	War Diary For September 1918 11th Bn. Royal Scots Fusiliers DAG 3rd Echelon		
Map	Map 2		
Miscellaneous	1.0 J.U.G.U		
Map	Map 3 Showing Dispositions.		
Map	Map		
Operation(al) Order(s)	11th Bn. Royal Scots Fusiliers. Operation Order No. 4.	28/09/1918	28/09/1918
Miscellaneous	Instructions No.1 To 59th Divisional Order No. 165	28/09/1918	28/09/1918
Operation(al) Order(s)	Addendum No 2 Operation Order No. 4.	29/09/1918	29/09/1918
Miscellaneous	Operations	01/10/1918	01/10/1918
Heading	War Diary Of The 11th Bn. Royal Scots Fus. For October 1918.		
War Diary	Cheltenham Road M 14 A 3.3.	01/10/1918	02/10/1918
War Diary	Pont Riqueul R3dl2 Bac St Maur G18C4.8	03/10/1918	06/10/1918
War Diary	Bac St Maur G18 C 48	07/10/1918	16/10/1918
War Diary	36/136 V J 31.	17/10/1918	18/10/1918

War Diary	Willems 37/M6.12	19/10/1918	19/10/1918
War Diary	Trieu de Wazon 37/N3.	20/10/1918	20/10/1918
War Diary	Houilly 37/M5	20/10/1918	20/10/1918
War Diary	Pont-A-Chin 37/132;126.	21/10/1918	22/10/1918
War Diary	Chaos	23/10/1918	31/10/1918
Map	Map		
Miscellaneous	Copy Of Operation Order Wired From Jugu To Paqu Sheet 36	14/10/1918	14/10/1918
Miscellaneous	Copy Of Situation Report Of Paqu To Jugu 18.00		
Miscellaneous	Copy Of Telegram From 178th Bde To This Unit BM 109		
Miscellaneous	Copy Of Bath Operation Order	16/10/1918	16/10/1918
Miscellaneous	Copy Of Wire From Jugu To Paqu	16/10/1918	16/10/1918
Miscellaneous	Copy Of Battn Operation Order 7	16/10/1918	16/10/1918
Miscellaneous	Copy Of Situation Report To Jugu 20.00	17/10/1918	17/10/1918
Operation(al) Order(s)	Extracts From 178th Bde Order No. 145	18/10/1918	18/10/1918
Miscellaneous	Extract From Battn Operation Order F627	17/10/1918	17/10/1918
Miscellaneous	Copy Of Situation Report Of Paqu To Jugu 1910	18/10/1918	18/10/1918
Miscellaneous	Copy Of Operation Orders Of 178th Bde	19/10/1918	19/10/1918
Miscellaneous	Copy Of Situation Report		
Miscellaneous	Copy Of Wires From Jugu to Paqu		
Miscellaneous	Copy Of Wires From Jugu to Paqu	21/10/1918	21/10/1918
Miscellaneous	Copy Of Battn Operation Orders	21/10/1918	21/10/1918
Miscellaneous	030815 19/10/18 Should 2nd 0815 20/10/18.		
War Diary	Chaos Forzeau H 25 C.d Sheet 36	01/11/1918	12/11/1918
War Diary	Velaines 37/K 13.	13/11/1918	14/11/1918
War Diary	Pecq 37/1.1.	15/11/1918	15/11/1918
War Diary	Willems 37/M5	16/11/1918	16/11/1918
War Diary	Pt Ronchin 36/Q 22.	17/11/1918	30/11/1918
Operation(al) Order(s)	178th Infantry Brigade Order No. 145.	04/11/1918	04/11/1918
Miscellaneous	Copy Of 178th Infantry Brigade Advance Instruction No. 1.	06/11/1918	06/11/1918
Miscellaneous	Operation Orders Of 178th Bde	10/11/1918	10/11/1918
Heading	11th. Royal Scots Fus. December 1918.		
War Diary	Petit Ronchin Sheet 36/922	01/12/1918	04/12/1918
War Diary	Bruay (44 B/J 16)	05/12/1918	07/12/1918
War Diary	Calonne Ricouart (44B/216)	08/12/1918	08/12/1918
War Diary	Dunkirk	09/12/1918	21/12/1918
War Diary	Dunkirk Hospice S. Pol Camp (Demobilization)	21/12/1918	31/12/1918
War Diary	Dunkerque Hospice Camp.	01/01/1919	01/02/1919
War Diary	Dunkirk	06/02/1919	28/02/1919
Heading	59 Division 178 Infantry Brigade 11 Battalion Royal Scots Fusiliers April To June 1919 Missing.		
War Diary	Dunkirk.	02/07/1919	26/07/1919

WO 3025

59th Div 178 INF Bde

11th BN Royal Scots Fus

1918 May – 1919 July

59TH DIVISION
178TH INFY BDE

11TH BN ROYAL SCOTS FUS.

MAY 1918 - JLY 1919

FROM UK

18/59

78a RS 11 Ger RS Army Form C. 2118.

I.E.

WAR DIARY
or
INTELLIGENCE SUMMARY
(Erase heading not required.)

Instructions regarding War Diaries and Intelligence Summaries are contained in F.S. Regs., Part II. and the Staff Manual respectively. Title pages will be prepared in manuscript.

Place	Date	Hour	Summary of Events and Information	Remarks and references to Appendices
	2.5.18		Strength of Battalion on Embarkation 29 officers 1077 Other Ranks (Total 1100). Left Dover Noon on the SS "Onward" disembarked at Calais, quartered in No 6 Rest Camp (East)	
	9.5.18		Batt'n passed through Base Gas Chamber	
	10.5.18	10.20pm	Entrained at Fontinettes (the Fontinettes) travelled overnight by rail (2 officers 100 OR left Battn for ETAPLES)	
	11.5.18		Arrived PERNES (AMBLAIN) marched to SAINS-LES-PERNES (the overnight travelling the march caused a fairly large proportion of men to fall out) Billeted in the Village	
	12.5.18		Travelled to AUCHEL by lorries. marched to CALONNE-RICOUART. Quartered in Huts & Tents. Placed in 178th K. Bde 59th Div	
	14.5.18		Commenced digging on B.B. line from Sheet 36 B.1.5.b8.2. — C.17.a.4.3	
	15.5.18		C.O 2/5th Sherwood Foresters ordered to get in touch with this Battn. & following officers of same unit 4 Company Commanders, Medical Officer & Quartermaster attached to unit for purpose of supervision. Medical Officer to visit this unit to help & advise.	
	15.5.18 17.5.18 18.5.18		Enemy shelled a line & neighbourhood (C.23 b central (36S)) with 15"(?) H.E. Casualties & damage — nil. Do Do Do portion of BB line allocated to this unit (CALONNE-RICOUART — MARLES-les-MINES Rd) In case of enemy attack running thro C.22.a (exclusive) to track running Reserve line on BB line (commenced digging Reserve line on BB line)	
	24.5.18 26.5.18		New frontage for this Batt'n from 1.6.d.7.2.(36S) to (origin at C.24.a.0.0 (36S) Move cancelled. New frontage C.19.a (36S) Railway incl. to 15 d railway excl.	
	27.5.18		Vacated camp which was taken over by Chinese Labour Batt'n 2 Coys quartered in der canvas 2 Coys billeted in building AT AUCHEL	

D. D. & L., London, E.C.
(A10256) Wt W5300/P713 750,000 2/13 Sch. 52 Forms/C2118/16

Army Form C. 2118.

WAR DIARY
or
INTELLIGENCE SUMMARY.
(Erase heading not required.)

Instructions regarding War Diaries and Intelligence Summaries are contained in F. S. Regs., Part II. and the Staff Manual respectively. Title pages will be prepared in manuscript.

Place	Date	Hour	Summary of Events and Information	Remarks and references to Appendices
	29/5/18		Marker company HT camp for Billet in AUCHEL	
	29/5/18	10p–1a	Aircraft Bombs fell near mens billet no damage or casualties	
	30/5/18	9.30am	4 8"(?) shells fell on left sector of our B.B. line (other shells fell on B.B line left of our sector) Officers attached to this bath for supervision cease to be attached	

Macmillan Maj. A. Lt.-Col.
Comdg 11th (Garr.) Bn. Royal Scots Fusiliers

CONFIDENTIAL.

WAR DIARY

of the

11th G G Bn. Royal Scots Fusiliers

from 1st June 1918 to 30th June 1918.

CONFIDENTIAL

D. A. G.

  3rd Echelon.

   WAR DIARY.

  Herewith copy of War Diary for month of June, 1918.

                              R P MacLachlan Lt.Col.,
                       Cmdg.,11th (Garr) Bn. Royal Scots Fusiliers

WAR DIARY
or
INTELLIGENCE SUMMARY.
(Erase heading not required.)

Army Form C. 2118.

Place	Date	Hour	Summary of Events and Information	Remarks and references to Appendices
AUCHEL	June 1918 2nd		Strength of Battalion — 29 Officers + 954 ORs	
			Batt'n manned "BB" defence line (C.24 a O.O. to 1.6 d 7.2 (44B/36B))	
	3rd		Commenced work of "BB" Reserve line (1.4 a + c 5.0 (44B))	
	6		This unit allotted new frontage in BB line. C.24 a O.O. to road and C.3 c 7.2 (44B)	
	8		Decrease in Strength. Lieut J.M. Leburn and 2 other ranks invalided to U.K., 2 other ranks killed (aircraft). 8 other ranks reclassified (Category A) posted 1st Bn R.S.F.	
	9	9am	Batt'n manned new sector of "BB" line. 7am — 11am. Hostile shelling of BB line + approaches. 2 Guns working together (2 10.5 cm (?) shells fell in vicinity of trench in C.23 a (44B), 12 15cm (?) shells in vicinity of X roads C.16 c 5.0 (44B). (Casualties nil).	
	13		65 Other ranks joined Battn from Base	
	16		Batt'n left AUCHEL marched to PRESSY les PERNES (Dist 8 Km)	
	17		Batt'n left PRESSY les PERNES marched to LISBOURG via FIEFS (dist. 18 Km).	
			On both days men marched in Battle Order; packs were carried by motor lorries. The second days march was a severe test. 130 other ranks fell out.	
LISBOURG	18.		Men in billets in farm buildings. Batt'n now engaged in Intensive Training for rest of month. Epidemic of "Fever" began to make itself felt. (Continued for remainder of month.) Practically all officers + other ranks fell victims	

Army Form C. 2118.

WAR DIARY
or
INTELLIGENCE SUMMARY.
(Erase heading not required.)

Instructions regarding War Diaries and Intelligence Summaries are contained in F. S. Regs., Part II. and the Staff Manual respectively. Title pages will be prepared in manuscript.

Place	Date	Hour	Summary of Events and Information	Remarks and references to Appendices
LISBOURG	24/6/18		2 officers draft & 19 other ranks sent to form 178 Bde Light T.M. Battery.	
	25/6/18		48 other ranks taken on strength with effect from 24/6/18 on arriving from Garrison Base Depot.	
			50 other ranks reclassified (categories B.ii & B.iii) proceeded to Garrison Base Depot & struck off strength.	
			Inspection by Corps Commander (X Corps)	
	30/6/18		Strength of Batt. — 28 Officers & 979 other ranks.	

R.R. Maclachlan............ Lt.-Col.
Comdg. 1/1 (Garr.) Bn. Royal Scots Fusiliers

CONFIDENTIAL

War Diary

of the

11th Bn. R. Scots Fusiliers

From 1st July 1918   To. 31st July 1918.

11 Royal Scots Fusiliers 1/7/1918

Army Form C. 2118.

WAR DIARY
or
INTELLIGENCE SUMMARY.

Place	Date	Hour	Summary of Events and Information	Remarks and references to Appendices
LISBOURG (Sheet 44c)	1.7.18		Strength of Battn. 28 officers 979 other ranks	
			Training of Batt'n continues, in area E.24.a (44?). — Tactical Schemes v Map Reading for officers P.T. v B.F, musketry including range work, Anti-Gas Training Arms Drill, Lewis Gun, Snipers & Scouts, Platoon v Company Drill. Battalion Drill v Route March (10-12 Km) once a week	
-do-	2.7.18		The following officers reported for duty & taken on strength of Batt'n. Capt. H.W. Howie, Capt. R. Patterson, 2/Lieut W.F. Fraser (all of Ayrshire Yeomanry) Lieut. P. Oakes, W.B. Hodge, W.R. Kennedy, F.K. Cowper, 2/Lieuts J. Sutherland G.B. Fleming (all of R. Scots Fus)	
			1 other rank struck off strength sick	
-do-	4.7.18		1 OR struck off strength sick	
DELETTE	5.7.18		Batt'n occupied practice trenches for 24 hours. proceeded to trenches by buses at 7.15 am. returned on 6.7.18 leaving trenches about 10 am. A & B occupied Observation & Front lines, 'C' in support & 'D' in reserve. 6 am. 'C' Coy relieved 'B' & 'D' relieved 'A' Coy from Hoop'	
			5 OR taken on strength from Hoop'. 2 OR struck off strength	
			2/Lieut P.T. Vaughan to be Acting Quartermaster	
LISBOURG	7.7.18		Capt. H.M. Barrand (3rd (Gm. Hrs) struck off strength (authority A.G. F.33/7 m.	
-do-	8.7.18		Capt W. Pettigrew (R. Scots Fus) reported & taken on strength of Batt'n. Demonstration of Platoon Drill by H.A.C. Demonstration Platoon	
	9.7.18		1 OR struck off strength sick	
	10.7.18		Batt'n inspected by Gen. Sir H.S. Horne KCB, KGMG	
	11.7.18			
	13.7.18		3 OR struck off strength (1 sick, 2 reclassified B₃)	

Army Form C. 2118.

WAR DIARY
or
INTELLIGENCE SUMMARY.
(Erase heading not required.)

Instructions regarding War Diaries and Intelligence Summaries are contained in F. S. Regs., Part II. and the Staff Manual respectively. Title pages will be prepared in manuscript.

Place	Date	Hour	Summary of Events and Information	Remarks and references to Appendices
LISBOURG (Sheet 44c)	15.7.18		3 ORs. struck off strength (1 sick 2 to UK for commissions)	
	17.7.18		Capt H.C. DICKENS (3rd E.Yorks) and 26 ORs reduced in category, & struck off the strength of Battn on proceeding to Corr Base Depot.	
	18/7/18		Capt A.N. TOOVEY (5th North'd Fus) reduced in category, & struck off strength of Battn on proceeding to Corr. Base Depot.	
			1 OR struck off strength sick	
	19/7/18		1 OR rejoined unit from Hosp & taken on strength.	
	20/7/18		1 OR — do —	
			— do —	
			Battn Badge 2" squares of Green cloth issued to all ranks worn on the sleeves.	
			A & B. Companies attacked to 55th Div for instruction in trench duties at 3·15pm. 2 Coys 336 all ranks embus at LISBOURG & debussed at F.28.6.6.(4·3) at 10pm. Guides conducted & Small parties of the two companies of 5th Bn, 6th Bn & 7th Bn Kings Liverpool Regt. holding GIVENCHY sector of front line	
	22/7/18		Companies ordered to embus at F.28.6.7.6.(4·9.8) at 12·30am but owing to companies being scattered so much this was not completed until about 3·15am. Casualties while visiting trenches 4 ORs killed, 11 ORs Wounded 4 men were left behind but rejoined on 23/7/18.	
	21/7/18		Capt. D.C. Brown 6/7 R Scots Fus. reported for duty & taken on strength.	
			One other rank — do —	
			Two — do — struck off strength sick	
	22/7/18		One — do — — do —	

Army Form C. 2118.

WAR DIARY
or
INTELLIGENCE SUMMARY

(Erase heading not required.)

Instructions regarding War Diaries and Intelligence Summaries are contained in F. S. Regs., Part II. and the Staff Manual respectively. Title pages will be prepared in manuscript.

Place	Date	Hour	Summary of Events and Information	Remarks and references to Appendices
LISBOURG	23/7/18		178th Bde moved in one convoy from FONTAINES les BOULANS at 1.30 pm. The 11th Bn. R. Scots Fus. marched to embussing point & debussed at BARLY (Lens 11.G.3/6.0)	
BARLY (Lens 11 G.3/6.0)	24/7/18		Billetted in East end of BARLY. Bn. Hdqrs. & 3 officers per company reconnoitred PURPLE LINE M.31, S.1, v S.2 (51B) Travelled by motor lorries to & from the trenches	
	25/7/18		3 ORs taken on strength, 2 OR struck off strength sick	
	29/7/18		Training programme as on 1/7/18 continued	
	30/7/18		Lt H R Thompson & Lt J D Panton struck off strength (178 Bde memo 702/4)	
	31/7/18		one OR struck off strength sick. Strength of Batt.n 31 officers 914 other ranks	

J S Mcmillan, Major
11th R.S. Fusiliers

CONFIDENTIAL.

WAR DIARY

OF

11th Royal Scots Fusiliers.

FOR

AUGUST, 1918.

Vol 4

H.E.I
5 sheets

Army Form C. 2118.

WAR DIARY
or
INTELLIGENCE SUMMARY.
(Erase heading not required.)

August 1918   11 Royal Irish Fusiliers

Instructions regarding War Diaries and Intelligence Summaries are contained in F. S. Regs., Part II. and the Staff Manual respectively. Title pages will be prepared in manuscript.

Place	Date	Hour	Summary of Events and Information	Remarks and references to Appendices
BARLY (51 c P 15)	Aug 1st		Strength of Battn. 31 Officers 944 ORs. Unit inspected by GOC 6th Corps.	
	Aug 2nd		Unit relieved the 26th R. Welsh Fusiliers in the BRICKFIELD strong point 51BSW/S a.3 D & B (Coys entrained on Light Railway at BAVINCOURT (51c 34 b) at 5.45 pm & 6.45 pm A & C Coys ——do—— ——do—— ——do—— Relief complete at 3.30 am 3/8/18. Detraining Point "MARBLE ARCH" (51BSW M 21 a 54). Dispositions as per attached sketch.	✗
BRICKFIELD Strong Pt 51B/S a.3	Aug 3rd	10 pm	Working party on MERCATEL SWITCH 250 men Battn. HQtrs. shelled during day one OR casualty.	
	Aug 4th	9 pm	Working party of 100 men on BOISLEUX Ave ——do—— ——d——100—— ——do—— MERCATEL SWITCH	
	Aug 5th	7 am	Enemy extremely quiet. Working party 1 off 11 OR dumping out S 3 a T 6. ——do—— ——do—— 1 NCO 10 OR PURPLE LINE ——do—— 1 off 100 OR MERCATEL SWITCH	
		9 "	——do—— 1 off 100 OR Railway Cut S 3 a	
		9.30 pm	Transport shelled at night. One OR wounded.	
	Aug 6th	7 am	Working party 1 off 100 OR S 3 a T 6	
		9 "	——do—— 1 NCO 10 OR R 36 a 53	
		"	——do—— 1 off 100 OR Railway Cut S 3 a	
		9.30 pm	——do—— 1 off 100 OR S 3 d T 5.	
		9.0 pm		

WAR DIARY

Army Form C. 2118.
Sheet 2

August 1918 — 1st Royal Inniskilling Fusiliers (?)

INTELLIGENCE SUMMARY

(Erase heading not required.)

Instructions regarding War Diaries and Intelligence Summaries are contained in F.S. Regs., Part II. and the Staff Manual respectively. Title pages will be prepared in manuscript.

Place	Date	Hour	Summary of Events and Information	Remarks and references to Appendices
BRICKFIELD Strong Point 51B/S2 v 3	Aug. 7 " 8 " 9 Aug 10th		Extremely quiet days. Very little shelling. Casualties nil. Weather fine & dry. Working parties as on 6th inst. Unit relieved 36th Bn North'd Fus. in front line system. Dispositions as per attached sketch.	
	" 11 " 12 " 13 " 14 " 17		Enemy activity much below normal. Casualties - nil. Weather - fine & dry. Inter-batt. relief. C & D Coys relieved A & B Coys in the Observation & Support Lines. Battn relieved by 2/6th Bn DURHAM L.I. Relief complete by 1.45 am.	
BARLEY 51c. P.15.	" 18		Battn embussed at 51c/R 33 69.4 in 2 convoys 3 am & 4.30 am debussed at BARLEY 51c P.15. Billeted in village.	
	" 19 " 20		Training. P.T. & B.F. A. Gas. Close order drill etc from 8.30 am - 12.30 pm. Recreation football in afternoon.	
	" 21		Battn embussed at 6.30 pm at FOSSEUX 51c P.10 proceeded to 51c R 33 69.4 & guided to Reserve line 51c X.3. Relief complete 11pm. Relieved 2nd Bn. SCOTS GUARDS	
	" 22 " 23.		Unit supplied guides to lead 1st Bn London Regt to Battle positions at BOISIEUX au MONT Battn marched from Reserve line 5 pm via BELLACOURT, BASSEUX, BAILLEULMONT, LAHERLIERE, arrived 10.30 pm. Bivouaced in field 51c V9 d 6.3	
	" 24		Entrained at SAULTY STATION 10.45 am. arrived BERGUETTE at 6 pm.	

Army Form C. 2118.

August 1918   WAR DIARY   1st Royal Scots Fusiliers
              or
              INTELLIGENCE SUMMARY.
              (Erase heading not required.)

Place	Date	Hour	Summary of Events and Information	Remarks and references to Appendices
HAM EN ARTOIS	21st Aug 18		Battn. billeted in HAM EN ARTOIS.	
36 A. O.	25		59th Div relieved 7th Divisional.	
	27		Battn. moved up to ASILE d'ALIENES at ST VENANT. (36 A P.Q.C.v.d.) by motor lorries.	
ST VENANT	28			
36 A.P.Q.C.v.d	29		Battn. continued training. P.T., B.F., Musketry, A-Gas, Patrolling, Close order.	
	30		"	
	31		"	
			Alteration in Strength during month. (a) Decrease	
	3/8/18		Lt.Col. R.P. Maclachlan proceeded to U.K. (DAG 1st. 1010)	
	4/8/18		2nd Lieut. A.P. Mahood " " U.K. AG/668/111 M.	
	15/8/18		2 Lieut. V.W. Wyatt " " U.K. 59 Div. A 100/53/144	
	17/8/18		Lieut G.R. Sharrock " " "MT TM.BY. AG/2158/5012.	
	22/8/18		Capt. D.C. Brown Lt. W.B. Hodge, Lt. D.E. Riley proceeded to Base Depot AG 2158/5340 (0)	
	27/8/18		2nd Lt. Doherty D. proceeded to Base Depot reclassification in category	
	30/8/18		Capt. H.G. Dickens BA " " " "	
	30/8/18		Capt. K.H. Rennie " " " "	
			(b) Increase	
	5/8/18		2nd Lieut C.P. Doly (3rd RSF) reported for duty & taken on strength.	
	10/8/18		Lt.Col. J.N. de la Perrelle DSO. MC. Bord Regt assumed command of Battn.	
	14/8/18		Lieut J Taylor (Lanarkshire Yeo) & 2/Lt J.H. Scott, A.W. McCall, W. Abson (RSF) taken on strength.	
	24/8/18		2/Lieuts T.H. Oakden. D.S.O. D.W. Matheson, N.C. Donaldson. H.J. Graham. A. Gilliat (7th Borders Regt.) taken on strength of battn.	

August 1918. WAR DIARY 11 Royal Scots Fusiliers
           or
       INTELLIGENCE SUMMARY.
         (Erase heading not required.)

Army Form C. 2118.

Place	Date	Hour	Summary of Events and Information	Remarks and references to Appendices
			Alteration of Strength (cont'd) : Other ranks.	
			(a) Decrease.	
			① Sick 32	
			② Wounded 6	
			③ U.K.(Commissions) 2	
			④ Other units 5	
			45	
			(b) Increase	
			① Returned from C.C.S. 15	
			② Reinforcements 13	
			28	
	Aug 3rd		Bath (in support Bde) moved up from ST VENANT to Junction Roads 36A/Q.11.b.7.1. All ranks in bivouacs in fields in immediate vicinity	

Signed J Grant
Lt Col
Comdg 11 Royal Scots Fusiliers

Confidential

War Diary

of

11ᵗʰ Royal Scots Fusiliers

September 1918.

WAR DIARY or INTELLIGENCE SUMMARY

Army Form C. 2118.

Place	Date	Hour	Summary of Events and Information	Remarks and references to Appendices
36A/Q.11 b 7.1	Sept 1 1918		Strength of Battn. 38 officers 897 O.R.	
			Battn. in shell holes etc at Junction Roads 36A/Q.11 b 7.1 (59th Division immediate 177th Bde in advance guard hastening retirement of the enemy 178th Bde in immediate support. 11th R. Scots Fus in support to 178th Bde)	
	"2nd"	6pm	Battn. moved forward to neighbourhood of RUE DELANNOY 36A/R.15 c 1.2. Men in old trenches and in fields.	
	"3rd"	8.30am	Battn. again moved forward to neighbourhood of the FOSSE POST 36A/R.22 a + c	
		10.10	'B' Coy ordered to move forward to support 36th Bn North Yks. They took up a position in RIEZ BAILLEUL POST 36/M 8 c. 178th Bde now in advance guard having relieved 177th Bde.	
	"4th"	10.00	Battn. less 1 coy moved forward to area of CLIFTON G POST 36A/R.18 c.	
	"5th"	6.45am	Battn. relieved 36th Bn North Yks. See disposition map. 'B' Coy rejoined Battn. Battn. Sector subjected to vigorous shelling throughout the day. Enemy apparently determined to hold on to AUBERS RIDGE for a time.	Map 1.
			A Coy (Right Front Coy) sent out patrol followed by comp. occupied Old British Front line 'B' Coy (left " ") held up by Enemy Light MGs + Snipers	
	6th		Enemy artillery active day + night.	
	7th		Bn. Hdqrs moved to 36/M.17 a 6.4. 'B' Coy occupied small portion of Old British Front line	
	8th		Patrol from Right Front Coy entered German Trenches + found them empty. (Enemy holding NOTION, NATCH NONSENSE Trenches. 36/M 25 a+b, N.20.c. as his main line of resistance with light MGs moving about in trenches to East	

WAR DIARY
INTELLIGENCE SUMMARY

Army Form C. 2118.

Place	Date	Hour	Summary of Events and Information	Remarks and references to Appendices
TRENCHES FAUQUISSART 36/M.18.	9.9.18	3.45 pm	Very heavy area 'strafe'. Try hostile artillery 77mm 105mm 150mm & 210mm Area affected 36/M 23 ab M.17 c v d, M.18 a.	
		10.0 pm	Patrol again entered Old German trenches & found trenches clear of enemy as far as the DISTILLERY 36/M.19 c.50.00. Batt. could have occupied these trenches, but owing to fact that Batt. on its right & left could not make any headway, it was considered inadvisable.	
"	10.9.18		Relieved by 11th Bn SUSSEX REGT, 176th Bde. Extremely dark night, raining, men completely tired & worn out. Relief not complete until 5.30 am.	
Corps Main Defence Line (PURPLE) and CORPS RES. DEFENCE LINE (RED DOTTED)	11.9.18		Batt. occupying billets, etc in Corps Main Defence Line and Reserve — see disposition	2
	12.9.18	2.30 am 4.10 am	Heavy Hostile artillery fire round Bn. Hdqrs at CHARTERHOUSE POST. Batt. Hdqrs moved to BOUT DEVILLE. (36ª/R.18C.32)	
36ª/R.18C.32	12.9.18 13.9.18 14.9.18 15.9.18 16.9.18 17.9.18 18.9.18		Unit engaged digging posts in Corps Defence & Reserve lines. see disposition D and C coys in Corps main Defence line A. " B. " " " Reserve " Scores of Rifles into cemented shell holes and L.G. posts, revetted and drained and duck-boarded with double Belts of wire thrown out zig-zag in front of shown and L.G. shoots to cover approaches and gaps. Work done at dusk between 6 and 8 p.m owing to facilities of enemy observation. Programme in daytime carried out by Coys separately — musketry and drill for short periods in small parties in orchards to avoid Enemy observation. Inspections. Bathing (Bn. baths fitted up at Bn. HQ (36ª/R.18C.3.2) Improvement of Billets and shelters, and Road making	2
	12.9.18 to 20.9.18		and ditching on roads in Bn. area (1st and 6th Sept) under R.E. supervision	

WAR DIARY or INTELLIGENCE SUMMARY

Army Form C. 2118.

Place	Date	Hour	Summary of Events and Information	Remarks and references to Appendices
BOUT DEVILLE	12/9/18 to 18/9/18		Salvage parties organised by Coys. each evening between 5.30 and 7 p.m. and material obtained taken to LESTREM by motor limbers.	
"	20/9/18		Lecture at Bde H.Q. to Platoon Comd⁹⁵ by G.S.O. 2 XI Corps. Subject "Intelligence". Lieut J EDWARD ROBSON I.O. left in evening to attend 3 weeks S.O.S. Course S.⁴Y. and handed over his duties to 2/Lt. A.J.D. PORTEOUS.	
		8 p.m 7.30 p.m		
"	19/9/18	8.30 pm to 11.30 pm	Practice "stand to" for the Bn. in battle positions ordered by G.O.C.	
"	20/9/18		Preparations for Bde tactical advance guard scheme, carried out on this date by 3/5 NORTHUMBERLAND FUSILIERS, to be carried out the following day by the 1/4 R.S. Fus. over same ground. (A16.7.18. M13 - Rly. LESTREM 36°52'2 1:10000. AUBERS 36 SW.) (1:10000)	
"	21/9/18		Scheme cancelled owing to stormy weather conditions. Advance Parties from each Platoon and Bn H.Q. went up in afternoon to reconnoitre front line sector previously held by us (RIGHT SECTOR) preparatory to a relief the following evening.	
N17@5.5	22/9/18	11.30 pm	Relieved the 1/4 SOMERSET LIGHT INFANTRY in the line (M17, 18, 23, 24, N13/36SW) No casualties. Relief completed by midnight. See DISPOSITION MAP.	3.
"	23/9/18		Evening patrols sent out by S.L.I. 9-11 p.m. 5 a.m to 5.15 am ("Stand to") and 6.0 am to 6.15 am. ("Stand down) — Heavy hostile shelling of front line. Hostile artillery very quiet during morning. More active during afternoon and evening. G.O.C. went round line from 10 am to 2.15 p.m. Visited A.C. and D Coys; and reconnoitred No Man's Land. 4.45 – 6.30 p.m – Daylight patrol from D Coy under 2/Lt R. H. McGRAW reconnoitred ROTTEN ROW (N186), trench (N13 d. 52 – N13d. 79) and portion of NE/SR TRENCH. Found them unoccupied but encountered rifle and m.G. fire. 9-10.30 p.m 2/Lt. D.W.H. MATHESON took out patrol from C. Coy to reconnoitre suspected enemy posts located enemy working party and 2 E.M.Gs in N19 a, c (NINEPIN TRENCH and TRIVELET sector.) Great Activity on both sides 5-7.30 p.m. One of our teams brought down in flames 5.15 p.m.	Coys. C - Purple trench D - Rifle trench A - Right Support B - Left Support

Army Form C. 2118.

WAR DIARY
or
INTELLIGENCE SUMMARY.
(Erase heading not required.)

Instructions regarding War Diaries and Intelligence Summaries are contained in F. S. Regs., Part II. and the Staff Manual respectively. Title pages will be prepared in manuscript.

Place	Date	Hour	Summary of Events and Information	Remarks and references to Appendices
M17c55	24:9:18	12.50m to 1.30 AM	Two special reconnoitring patrols sent out from C coy under CAPT. P. DALE and 2/Lt W. ABSON to reconnoitre & suspected M.G. positions confirmed several & these and established the fact that W side of FAUQUISSART ROAD strongly held with MG's	
	"	5am – 8.30 PM	G.O.C. 59th DIVISION with I.T.O. went round front line (RIGHT SECTOR) and made personal reconnaissance	
	"	8.30 — to 2am.	Great aerial activity on both sides in afternoon and evening especially 5.30–7 p.m. Operation carried out by 2 platoons of D coy to extend left flank along road B. this line in N13d to N13a 9098 and thence down NORTHUMBERLAND AVENUE to junction with trenches in front of RUE TILLELOY met by heavy MG fire between ROTTEN ROW and NORTHUMBERLAND AV. and had to withdraw after establishing night posts at FISHTAIL and RED LAMP CORNER (N13d) to O.B. front line which they occupied will hold & 5am as 5. end of ROTTEN ROW.	
	24:9:18	6 /m 9.15 /m	C coy sent out patrol which reconnoitred NINE PIN TRENCH finding it unoccupied but encountering MG fire. Other patrols sent out later confirmed information as to location of MG's	
	25:9:18	12.50 am – 1.50 AM	2 LT CONNELLY took out a patrol from A coy to reconnoitre east of enemy wire from N19a5.2 to N19 d 2.2 unable from our trenches in D coy's sector. Reported on formidable nature of the belt and presence of waterlogged trenches and ditches 100" in front of wire.	
	"		Our artillery and aircraft very active during day. Operation carried out by Division on our right (19th) in early morning. Length of trench dug during night of 24/25 Sept opening up C.T. to MOTTES TRENCH. Leaving 0.12 front line at M24 d 3.7.	
	"	2.15 pm	3 Huns spotted by our observers at M13 d 3 3 aping constructing M.G. emplacement. Heavy hostile shelling & suspect back areas during night of 25/26th Sept, especially MUSSELOT, WANGERIE, and ROAD BEND POSTS and Bn.H.Q. (M17,18.)	
	"	10 pm	2/Lt J. SUTHERLAND took out a patrol from C coy and found MOTTES TRENCH unoccupied.	

Army Form C. 2118.

WAR DIARY
or
INTELLIGENCE SUMMARY.
(Erase heading not required.)

Instructions regarding War Diaries and Intelligence Summaries are contained in F.S. Regs., Part II. and the Staff Manual respectively. Title pages will be prepared in manuscript.

Place	Date	Hour	Summary of Events and Information	Remarks and references to Appendices
M17 c 5.5	26.9.18	12.15 am to 1.20 am	2/Lt N.C. DONALDSON took out a patrol from A Coy to corroborate the information concerning enemy wire in N19a obtained the previous evening. He reconnoitred the wire from N19a 6.2 (TRIVELET) to N19a 9.9 (Our Line) and confirmed the defenders as to the obstacle being 30' deep and 5" high on the road and on average 20' elsewhere. Also confirmed reports of disused bundles and several waterlogged ditches in front. Overneath investigated 5' wire belt on southern side of FAUQUISSART ROAD in N19c.	
		9.30 am	Smoke Screen erected on CORPS front but no information obtained of its existence by direct observation from PEAK O.P. (M22b 80 55)	
		10.0 am – 2 pm	Advance party from D. of W. SHROP. RIDING REGT came to reconnoitre line. Our artillery (6") busy cutting wire all morning on front of DIVISION on right.	
		7 pm (27.9.18)	9th Welsh W. RIDINGS relieved our two front Coys and Bn.HQ and our right supports Coy. Our Bn relieved our B Coy in left Supports being temporarily attached from the Batn. A.B. and C Coys came back to OUTPOST RESERVE LINE. A Coy — LAVENTIE EAST Area M 6.11.12, 14.2 B Coy — F—a L'ÉPINETTE " M 6 b d C Coy — HAILLYBOURG RD and LA FLINQUE POST Area M 15b 1.2	
LA BASSÉE RD M14d 9595 (near Govt men) to	27/9/18 to 29.9.18	7.50 – 9.30 am	2/Lt J.D. DEAS Bn. HQ – LA BASSÉE RD M14d 9595' Best Boy took out patrol and reccd NAVY TRENCH and area N13a.8. Returned ground very broken from A. B. C Coys in billets in trifurcation for intending attack, but was woken upon and gets located BENG. B Coy in support as 15th W. RIDINGS in MASSELOT (1+2) and old B. SUPPORT LINE (trench M 12 d 4) to N12a 51 to M12c 85.) Heavy shelling in M15 (especially B Coy billets) during 28th and 29th.	
	28/29 9.18	night	2/Lt V.H. SCOTT took out patrol to reconnoitre enemy wire from M19a 6.2 to N19a 7.3 and returned with report of artillery in cutting it. Report Barricades wire destroyed in several places.	
M17c 5.5	29/30 9.18	night	Relieved D.o.W.'s in the line who left 2 coys in support line under orders of CO. 11th RGT all coys 9 11th RGT took up positions in front line, reconnoitred by Pl.Cdrs & seen correctly in the afternoon day as furnishing off parties.	

WAR DIARY
INTELLIGENCE SUMMARY

Army Form C. 2118.

Place	Date	Hour	Summary of Events and Information	Remarks and references to Appendices
N17c.5.5.	30/9/18	7.30 pm ZERO.	At 7.25 p.m. the Bn "attacked with B Coys on the front from N13c 8.8 to N24d 2.7 under a covering barrage of artillery T.M.B. and M.G. fire which opened at zero on the intermediate objective (7.30.0 am). The intermediate and final objectives were taken on time and from observation was made from the enemy M.O.'s & artillery fire under if shells fire coys was:- A coy on the centre B coy on the left C on the right D coy formed a left defensive flank. On reaching the final objective Coys commenced to dig in and consolidate just in rear and were engaged on this for most of day. Enemy snipers began their activity when the barrage died down at 8.30 a.m. and remained very troublesome all day, causing many of the casualties. At 10 am one of our posts having advanced too far, in N13c 7.7 was surrounded by 30 or 40 of the enemy and forced to surrender after being several men. Average depth of advance 650' on frontage of 1800'. Considerable damage in personnel was done to the enemy and one Light M.G. Cast'rad and 1. "B" Coy Prisoners of War captured. 19. Our Casualties. 3 Officers 2/Lt F. Teames and 2/Lt A.W. McCall "B" Coy Prisoners 2/Lt J.D. Bers wounded O.R. Killed 8 / Died of wounds 3 / Died of wounds 23 / missing 16 / wounded 23 / The Baln (minus 1 Plat Q.1 Sec'n of 'D' coy) was relieved by 2 Bns. 7th Div. 28 & 1/7th D.W., which dressed the B.W. Brigade between them, into B.W. Boundary. Guard line dividing :- M.18, N13 from M24. N19. 15th Essex relieved our D and B coys with 2 coys in new outpost line 2 peats in old front line and 2 peats. in sect B support line. The relief not being complete by daylight, 1 Plat. 2/L sec 'B' coy could not be relieved and following night and O.C. Ry (Capt OAKDEN) remained all day as coy H.Q. in front line, the 2/6 D.L.I relieved our A and C coys until similar dispositions. Belily com- the 2/6 D.L.I relieved our A and C coys until daylight. H.Q. at MAIN POST (M22 d 4.7)	See Map 3 for new line etc and L.O's intro on operations attached
	30/9/18 - 1/10/18	night		

WAR DIARY
INTELLIGENCE SUMMARY.

Army Form C. 2118.

Place	Date	Hour	Summary of Events and Information	Remarks and references to Appendices
	Sept 1918		ALTERATION OF STRENGTH during month.	
			I – Officers :- (a) Increase :-	
H.Q.	1/9/18		2/Lt W. CONNELLY "A" Coy – Posted from Base and taken on strength.	
	2/9/18		2/Lt A.I.D. PORTEOUS "B" Coy. – do	
	10/9/18		2/Lt R.A. M'GRAW "D" Coy. – do	
	11/9/18		Lt C.S. MURRAY "C" Coy. – 3rd R. Scots. Returned & taken on strength.	
			Capt A.B. NAYLOR "A" Coy. – 5th Notts & Derby. Taken on strength and to continue in employment as Cmdt 64th Div. Schl. (Auth :- A.G. 2168/4732(0) d 17:9:18.)	
	16/9/18		2/Lt W. ASTON "C" Coy. – Taken on strength on rejoining from Hospital.	
	19/9/18		Lt R.C. PATERSON "D" Coy. – Returned from XI Corps Gas School.	
			2/Lt DAVIS "A" Coy. – do	
	20/9/18		2/Lt D. MATHESON "C" Coy. – Returned from 5th Army musketry camp.	
	21/9/18		2/Lt SCOTT "A" Coy. – Returned Corps Gas School.	
	22/9/18		2/Lt J.D. DEAS "B" Coy. – 8th Border Regt. Returned & taken on strength.	
	24/9/18		2/Lt SUTHERLAND "C" Coy. – Returned from XI Corps L.G. School.	
			(b) Decrease :-	
	2/9/18		Lt B. CAMPBELL "C" Coy. – Evacuated to U.K. 21.8.18 and struck off strength accordingly, by order 5.9.18.	
	7/9/18		2/Lt G.C.D. JONES – Proceeded to U.K. and struck off strength. Auth : G.H.Q. List no 2436. 5/9/18 In orders 7/9/18.	
	8/9/18		2/Lt R.T. FARRER "D" Coy. – attached G.H.Q. for employment as conducting officer.	
	4/9/18		2/Lt ASTON – "C" Coy. – Struck off strength wounded.	
	5/9/18		2/Lt SUTHERLAND "C" Coy. – Proceeded to XI Corps L.G. School.	

WAR DIARY
or
INTELLIGENCE SUMMARY.

Army Form C. 2118.

(Erase heading not required.)

Instructions regarding War Diaries and Intelligence Summaries are contained in F.S. Regs., Part II. and the Staff Manual respectively. Title pages will be prepared in manuscript.

Place	Date	Hour	Summary of Events and Information	Remarks and references to Appendices
	2/8/18		2/Lt W.G. FRASER B'Coy posted to F.F. on B 178 Bde 21.8.18 Auth. A.G. 2158/5354 (0)	
	6/9/18		2/Lt G.B. FLEMING D Coy. Proceeded to 5th Army Infantry School.	
	9/9/18		LT H. J. HOWIE B Coy Struck off strength wounded	
	10/9/18		LT A.B. SADLER. O/r R.H. at 11th RSF. Struck off strength. Auth G.H.Q. Lor 1255/d.17/9/18. 3/6.m.	
	17/9/18		2/LT A GILLIAT D Coy proceeded for duty to U.K. and struck off strength accordingly Auth AG 116/143 (c)	
	19/9/18		LT. J EDWARD ROBSON 9.O. proceeded to E.g.g. at 5th Army S.O. & School.	
			2/LT W. ROBSON 'C' Coy – Struck off strength wounded.	
	25/9/18		2/LT " ISAACS } B Coy Killed in action	
			2/LT A.W. McCALL	
	30/9/18		2/LT J.D. DEAS . B Coy . Struck off strength – wounded.	
			1: Other Ranks.	
			(A) Increase.	
			① Returned from Hospital 29	
			② " Courses 21	
			③ " detention 2	
			other units 9c. 5	
			④ Reinforcements ___	
			Total 57	
			(B) Decrease	
			① Killed in action 22	
			② Missing 10	
			③ Died of wounds 5	
			④ Wounded 48	
			⑤ Sick – to Hospital 70	
			⑥ To courses 58	
			⑦ To Bde Command 9c. 15	
			⑧ To U.K. Special Reserve 1	
			Total 241	

War Diary for September 1918
11th Bn. Royal Scots Fusiliers

Original

DAG
3rd ECHELON

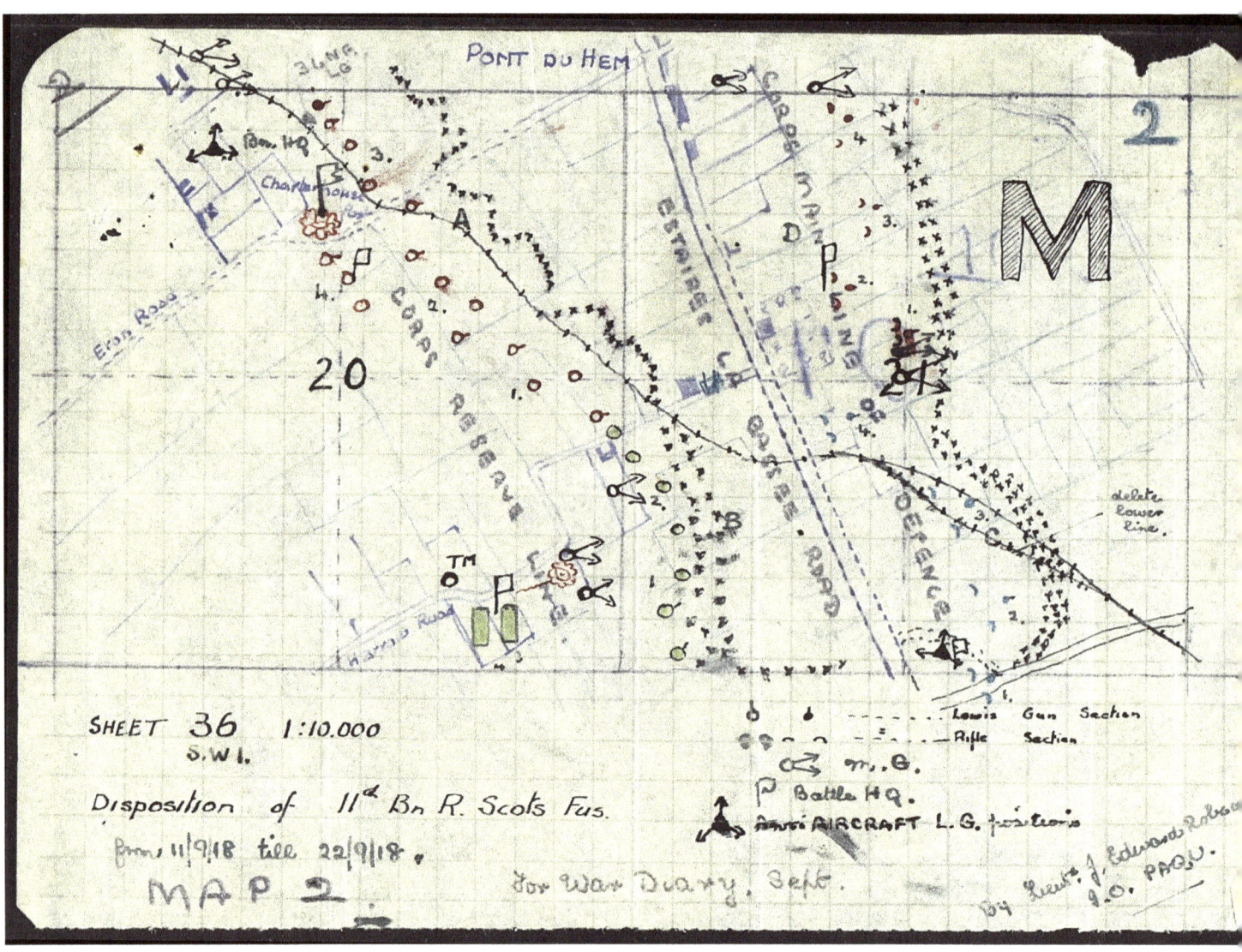

SHEET 36 1:10,000
S.W.1.

Disposition of 11th Bn R. Scots Fus.
from 11/9/18 till 22/9/18.
MAP 2.

For War Diary Sept.

By Lieut. J. Edwards Robson
I.O. PAGE.

1/1st Bn. R. Scots. Fus.

Positions showing

A. As handed over by 26th North'd Fus. 5.9.15
B. As obtained on 5.9.15
C. As handed over to 17th R Sussex Regt. 10.9.15

SHEET 36 1:20,000

SECRET   Copy No...8...

11th Bn. Royal Scots Fusiliers.

Operation Order No. 4.

Ref. Map - AUBERS 36 S.W.1.

1. 11th Bn. Royal Scots Fusiliers, in conjunction with the Unit on its right, will capture and hold the Line shown in Red on Map "A" attached, on Monday Sept. 30th, 1918.

2. Three Companies of 13th Duke of Wellington's West Riding Regiment will be in reserve under the orders of O.C., 11th Bn. Royal Scots Fusiliers.

3. The right boundary of the 11th Bn. Royal Scots Fusiliers, will be the GRID LINE between Squares M.24 and M.30 Eastwards.

4. Disposition for the attack is as follows:-
    "C" Coy., on right.
    "A" Coy., in centre.
    "B" Coy., on left.
Companies will attack on a two Platoon front in two waves. The first wave to capture the intermediate objective, the second wave to leapfrog them on this new objective and capture the final objective
    "D" Coy., will establish a defensive flank on left.
    Company boundaries are as shown in Green on Map attached.

5. After capturing final objective, patrols will be pushed forward close up to the protective barrage, and every effort will be made to mop up CLARA'S FAN.

6. A Liaison Post will be formed before the attack at M.24.d.1.2 under the command of an officer of the right battalion O.C., Coy., will detail one intelligent N.C.O. with one rifle section for this post.

7. On completion of their barrage programme two sections of "A" Coy., 25th Bn. M.G.Corps, and four light trench mortars of 178th L.T.M.Battery, will come under orders of O.C., 11th Bn. Royal Scots Fusiliers for consolidation purposes.

8. Artillery programme is as follows:-
    From Zero to Zero plus 5 field artillery will fire H.E. on all targets West of the intermediate objective, and shrapnel on all other targets
    From Zero plus 5 to Zero plus 25 field artillery will fire H.E. on all targets.
    From Zero plus 25 all 18 pounders will fire shrapnel and H.E. mixed on the protective barrage line. One round smoke to 5 rounds H.E.
    From Zero plus 30 all howitzers will fire on protective barrage line. One round smoke to 5 rounds H.E.
    At Zero plus 65 the protective barrage will commence to die down.
    At Zero plus 95 all field artillery fire will cease.
After this our fire will only open again in response to a call for S.O.S.. The S.O.S. line will be the same as the protective barrage line.

9. Directly the protective barrage lifts, patrols must be put out at once in front to get in touch with the enemy.

P.T.O.

-2-

10.   a. At <u>Zero plus 60</u> a conducting aeroplane is to fly over the front and call for Infantry positions by sounding a Klaxon Horn, and firing a white very light. Only the leading wave of infantry will acknowledge, promptly, by lighting red flares and flashing tin discs. If enemy counter attacks an aeroplane will fly over an hour or two after when troops will, when called upon, light their flares.

    b. The markings on the conducting aeroplane will be a square square black flap on the rear edge of the lower planes.

    A sharp look-out will be kept for low flying hostile aircraft. Rifle fire will be brought to bear immediately such a target is offered.

11.   A distinctive grenade will be fired by each platoon commander on reaching the final position allotted to his platoon.
    FINAL OBJECTIVE - Blue Ball.

12.   Watches will be synchronised at Battalion Headquarters - M.17.c.Central- at 3-0 p.m., and 11-0 p.m., 29/9/18.

13.   On the evening after the attack, the 467th Field Coy., R.E., and one company of the Pioneer battalion, will dig the following communication trenches.-
1. Existing trench from M.24.d.25.65 to M.24.d.6.3. will be improved and the old trench from the latter point to M.24.d.65.15 will be cleared.
2. Junction of MASSELOT STREET and the present line to N.19.a.6.8.
3. Front line at present held by posts from N.13.c.7.9. to RED LAMP CORNER.
   On completion of these, a further trench will be dug from N.13.c.65.85 to N.13.d.0.4.

14.   Zero hour will be notified later.

15.   Addendum No.1. attached (Instructions No.1 to 59 Divisional Order No.165) will be carefully explained to platoon commanders and all section leaders.
   Addendum No.2. (Administrative Instructions) attached.
   Addendum No.3 (Zero hour) attached.

16.   Acknowledge.

                                          Capt.
28/9/18.   Adjt. 11th Bn. Royal Scots Fusiliers.

<u>Copies to</u>:- 1. Commanding Officer.
         2. O.C., "A" Coy.,
         3. O.C., "B" Coy.,
         4. O.C., "C" Coy.,
         5. O.C., "D" Coy.,
         6. Intelligence Officer.
         7. File.
         8. War Diary.
         9. 178th Infy. Bde.
        10. O.C., 4th Shropshire L.I.
        11. 13th West Riding Regt.
        12. 36th Northumberland Fus:.
        13. O.C., 25th Bn. M.G.Corps.
        14. O.C., 178th L.T.M.Battery.

SECRET.

Copy No 8.

59th Div.
S.G. 3-11-6

176th Inf. Bde
177th   do
178th   do
25th Bn. M.G. Corps

INSTRUCTIONS No.1 to 59th DIVISIONAL ORDER No.165

1. ASSAULT FORMATIONS.

   The attack will be delivered by troops in either of the following formations:-

   (a) Lines of waves; each Company being on a 2 platoon frontage.
   (b) Columns of Platoons in Artillery Formation.
       It is not necessary that these columns should be in successive regular lines.
       On the contrary, sections should not be deployed until they come under fire.

2. (a) The situation which calls for the greatest initiative on the part of all is when one unit makes headway while the units on its flanks are checked.
   It then becomes the duty of every Officer and man to hold on at all costs and take steps to safe-guard the flanks.
   In this manner they will assist the units on their flanks which are checked.
   If the unit is distributed in depth (as it should be) a portion of the troops in the rear should be moved to the exposed flank to cover the gap.
   If there are no old trenches available every advantage should be taken of existing shell-holes for cover.

   (b) Men should be instructed beforehand to open fire on any target that presents itself during the advance without waiting for orders.
   They should take snap shots as 'guns' do when working with beaters.
   The fullest use should be made of the 36 Rifle Discharger Grenade.
   In this way the enemy will be prevented from bringing his M.Gs into action at fresh points.
   Throughout, good skirmishing, good leadership, and initiative, are essential.

3. As soon as the final objective has been captured and the situation permits, the troops should be thinned out.
   Those withdrawn should bring back casualties.
   Special men should be detailed to make stops in the trenches.

4. A definite task should be allotted to each man and his line of advance pointed out to him.
   Junior regimental officers should have the natural features and objects on their line of advance carefully pointed out to them.

5. INFORMATION: The rapid collection and transference of all information is of vital importance.
   (a) All men sent to the rear on duty of any kind should be given the latest information.
       If a message is of great importance or urgency it should be sent in duplicate.
       If one means of communication fails another should be tried.

(b) Contact patrols will be in the air, and when called upon, the infantry will communicate their position to them by means of ground flares or tin discs.

(c) To denote the fact that the assaulting troops have taken their objectives, special "success" signals will be used of either Very lights or coloured rifle grenades.

(d) Information will also be collected from the walking wounded by officers detailed previously for this work (At R.A.P.) In weighing the value of such information, due regard must be given to the mental condition of a wounded man.

(e) The points of junction with formation on flanks should send back all available information regarding the situation of neighbouring units.

(f) It should become a "habit" to send back frequent reports either of positive or negative information
Information should always be circulated both ways.

6. (a) MOPPERS-UP. Moppers-up will search all trenches, pill-boxes and shell-holes in their area. The German for "Hands up" is "Hando auf" (pronounced "Hender ouf")

(b) CARRYING PARTIES. Part of each attacking Company should be detailed as carrying parties, to bring forward picks, spades, food, water, ammunition, etc.

7. DRESS.

    Officers. All Company Officers will be dressed and equipped as the men; the platoon officers will carry rifles.

    Men. Attention is drawn to S.S. 135, Section XXXI, para 2.
Having due regard to the category of the men of the Division, care will be taken not to overload them. All Battalions of a brigade must be uniform in this respect.

8. The number of Officers and men to be left out of action will be in accordance with S.S. 135, sec.XXX. Officers and men at Schools or courses may be included in the total left out of action.

9. EQUIPMENT.

    Periscopes. Periscopes properly camouflaged must be carried by the assaulting troops.
The necessity for this is illustrated in a recent operation of the Division on our right. The advanced posts were kept under a close M.G. fire and the enemy crept up under cover without being detected.
It should be noted that the enemy makes great use of ditches in order to infiltrate forward to assemble for a counter-attack.

    Compasses. Compasses should be carried by all Officers who should verify the line of advance immediately previous to the attack.
The error of all compasses must be carefully checked as the steel helmet and box respirator affect them.

    BOMBS. All men of the rifle section will carry four bombs It must be ensured that all bombs are detonated beforehand.
All reinforcements should take up bandoliers and buckets of bombs

10. SALVAGE.

The equipment and rifles of all casualties will be collected and form a reserve.
Spare rifles will be cleaned and made available to replace rifles that have jambed or work stiff from overheating and dirt.
The provision of rifle oil is therefore important.
When the situation permits the cleaning of these rifles should be carried out by men working in pairs.
Enemy rifles, S.A.A. and bombs should be salved and used.

                    (Sgd) R.S. Follett,

                            Lt-Colonel,
28-9-18   G.S. 59th Division.

SECRET.
                                                    Copy No....8....

           A D D E N D U M No.2.   -   Operation Order No.4.

                        Administrative Instructions.

1.   4 Grenades. No.36, per man will be issued.

        Wire cutters will be issued to every second man.

        Shovels will be issued in every second man.

        1 tin disc, 1 red ground flare, and 1 very light will
        be issued to every man.

        1 S.O.S. rocket, and 1 blue ball grenade will be issued
        to platoon commanders.

             The above have been issued to Companies to-night.

        1 Bandolier additional to 120 rounds of S.A.A. carried on
        the man.

2.   S.A.A. etc., dumps have been formed as follows:-

                     M.24.d.3.7.
                     N.13.c.1.3.
                     N.13.c.4.6.

        These dumps will each contain :-
                     24 boxes S.A.A.
                     64 L.G. drums.
                     16 boxes L.G. ammunition.
                     6 boxes No.36 Grenades.
                     6 S.O.S. grenades.

        Dump at M.24.d.3.7. will have additional 32 boxes No.36 g
        grenades.

             These dumps will be formed by the 13th West Riding
        Regiment, and will be covered over with either a trench
        shelter or corrugated iron.
             Grenades will be detonated.

3.   R.E. dumps will be formed as follows:-
                     1. M.24.d.2.6.
                     2. M.13.c.1.3.
                     3. N.13.c.Central.
        Each of above will contain - duckboards, shovels, picks
        and 16 tins of water.
        Dump at N.13.c.1.3. will in addition have 3 planks 15 ft. 1
        long for bridging RIVERIE des LAIES.

4.   Regimental Aid Post will be at ROAD BEND POST - M.18.c.4.0
        Additional R.A.P. under M.O. of 13th West Riding Regt.
        will be at TRENCH FOOT CENTRE M.17.c.7.0.

                                                          Capt.
28/9/18.   Adjt. 11th Bn. Royal Scots Fusiliers.

S E C R E T   Copy No.... 8

A D D E N D U M No.3   -   Operation Order No.4.

Zero hour will be at 7-30 a.m.,

                                                    [signature]

                                                                  Capt.
29/9/18.   Adjt. 11th Bn. Royal Scots Fusiliers.

Information obtained as result of operation carried out by 11th Bn. ROYAL SCOTS FUSILIERS on morning of 30th September 1918.

OPERATIONS.

ENEMY RESISTANCE.

On opening of our Barrage enemy put up S.O.S. signals all along his line and well back.
Enemy resistance to our attacking troops - Practically NIL
Two guns fired isolated bursts.
In some cases Gunners abandoned their Machine Guns and fled;- Thirty or Forty gunners observed.
Hostile Artillery fired only a few shells; .77 calibre H.E. and Shrapnel.

OUR ADVANCE.

Our Barrage effective - that of our Machine Guns being especially so. Several casualties caused by our own shells, due either to short bursts or over keenness of the men which prompted them to advance too close up to it. Rate of Barrage pronounced by all to be rather slow in spite of the fact that ground to be traversed was pitted with shell holes interlaced with wire and intersected with waterlogged trenches and ditches. Our T.M.B. are also reported as having fired short. Intermediate objective gained on time, and second wave passing through first reached approximate line of final objective without serious opposition and commenced digging in. Some casualties during these operations. One section having advanced too far lost touch and ran into a nest of thirty of the enemy, who killed two and forced remainder to surrender. This occurred at approximately N.13d 7-7.

HOSTILE RETALIATION.

At zero plus 40 our barrage diminished in intensity and enemy commenced to shell approximately the line of RUE TILLELOY with 4-2's and 5-9's. Shooting ill-aimed and erratic. Hostile machine guns from the front and left flank also began to fire bursts at intervals - one in neighbourhood of PICANTIN, at approximately N.7d Central, especially troublesome.
At zero plus 60 enemy snipers commenced their activity, which continued for the rest of the day, rendering communication with the advanced line almost impossible.
About zero plus 90 enemy attempted to dribble forward men on left flank and bomb one of our posts about N.13d 5-8, but was driven back by Lewis Gun fire, which killed at least three.

SUBSEQUENT OPERATIONS.

Enemy very quiet for rest of day, with exception of activity of hostile snipers. One officer took out a patrol on left flank into vicinity of NEAR TRENCH, N.13d, but encountered opposition from Machine Guns and snipers, killing him and forcing the rest to withdraw.
T.M.Battery pushed forward guns into advanced line on request to strengthen defence.
Three Companies of 15th Duke of Wellington's West Riding Regiment moved forward into old British front line as support in case of counter attack.
LIASON POSTS, with 19th Division (Shropshire Regt) on Right established at N.19c 3-0 and N.19c 4-2 in neighbourhood of DISTILLERY (N.19c). Forward LIASON POST was to be established later in the evening at N.19c 8-0

OPERATIONS - continued.

RESULTS.
Line advanced on an average depth of 650 yards on frontage of 1800 yards.
Casualties light considering nature of operation - mostly leg and foot wounds.

CAPTURES.

PERSONNEL.
Prisoners (wounded and unwounded) approximately TEN.

MATERIAL.
One Light Machine Gun.

MISCELLANEOUS.
During the attack a lack of S.A.A. was experienced and difficulty of supplying troops in firing line considerable. Blue flares issued to platoon commanders rendered useless owing to defective detonators.

INTELLIGENCE.

Considerable enemy movement about "H" of NEAR TRENCH and in MOOSE TRENCH.

PRISONERS CAPTURED.
Prisoners captured report enemy line of resistance in NOTION, NATCH and NONSENSE trenches. Held by three Companies with one pushed forward in BERTHA TRENCH and neighbourhood. They are Saxons and report Prussians to be on their right

A patrol pushed forward from CLARA'S FAN reported enemy in considerable numbers, approximately sixty, in and around wooden huts which lie along line of trenches from N.19b 8-0 to N.20a 1-2.

A Machine Gun sniper still fires from RIFLEMAN'S AVENUE and enemy are also supposed to be in NORTHUMBERLAND AVENUE.

Alex. J. D. Porteous 2/85
A.O. 11th R.S.F.
2.10.18.

Map ref: AUBERS. 36 S.W.1. $\frac{1}{10000}$

1st Octr, 1918.

CONFIDENTIAL

WAR DIARY

of the

11TH BN. ROYAL SCOTS FUS.

for.

October 1918.

WAR DIARY 11/Royal Scots Fusiliers

INTELLIGENCE SUMMARY.

Army Form C. 2118.

(Erase heading not required.)

Place	Date	Hour	Summary of Events and Information	Remarks and references to Appendices
CHELTENHAM ROAD M.14.a.3.3.	1.10.18		Strength of Bn. 30 Officers 713 O.R. On relief by 15th ESSEX REGT and 2/6th D.L.I. Batn (less 1 Plat & Sect) Bn moved & relieved & proceeded to billets in CHELTENHAM ROAD (M.14.A). Remaining Platoon and Section of 17th un I.O. and section of B Coy relieved and rejoined Bn.	
PONT RIQUEUL a.c.8.m. R.3.d.4.2.	2.10.18	4 a.m. 8 p.m.	Bn. moved to PONT RIQUEUL (36.N.E.2/R.10.A) to billets vacated by 36th N.F. Co. Bn. H.Q. at R.3.d.4.2.	
BAC ST MAUR B.11.0.11.0. G.18.c.4.8.	3.10.18		Bn marched from billets at CONT RIQUEUL through LA GORGUE, ESTAIRES and SAILLY SUR LA LYS to BAC ST MAUR (36.N.W.) Brigade order forbidding troops entering towns on dugouts recently vacated by the enemy and Bn.H.Q. and Coys quartered in improvised shelters in the open. Coy areas as follows:— A Coy. FORT ROMPU H.8.c.2.5 B Coy. TWENTIETH POST M.14.a.2.0. Bn H.Q. G.18.c.4.8. C Coy. H.19.a.9.7. D Coy. YORK POST H.13.c.5.1	
	4.10.18 to 10.10.18		Period of Rest and Programme of Training carried out — Musketry, Bomb. C.T., Training & exercises in Rifle Grenade Shooting, L.G., Stretcher Bearing, and & Saluting and T.S. Rifles. Salvage parties organised daily. Baths and clean change of men. Portion of time devoted to improvement of billets which were passed as safe, and construction of adequate shelters and bivouacs. Invariant and details from LESTREM rejoined Bn. on 3rd inst. and remained with us during period. Bn Canteen Institute and Baths established in vicinity of FACTORY, BAC ST MAUR (H.13.c.25.85). No interference from hostile artillery. Hostile aircraft over our lines daily.	
	6.10.18	12:00	Inspection of Bn. by G.O.C. 178th Bde at G.18.c.68 who congratulated them on afternoon of 30th.	
			B Coy moved Bn. in area to vicinity of H.13.d.5.3.	

Army Form C. 2118.

11 Royal Scots Fusiliers

WAR DIARY
or
INTELLIGENCE SUMMARY.
(Erase heading not required.)

Instructions regarding War Diaries and Intelligence Summaries are contained in F.S. Regs., Part II. and the Staff Manual respectively. Title pages will be prepared in manuscript.

Place	Date	Hour	Summary of Events and Information	Remarks and references to Appendices
BAC ST MAUR G.12 c 4.8.	7:10:18	2000 to 2230	Runners for all officers of the Bn. at Bn H.Q. in commemoration of the successful operation of 30th Sept. carried out by the 11th R. Scots Fusiliers	
	8:10:18	1530 1730	Divisional Band played to Bn. at Bn. H.Q. Lieut J. Edward Robson returned from 5th Army S.O.S. course and resumed his duties as Intelligence Officer.	
	10:10:18		Batn. moved into Bde support the Bde having taken over the right sector of the Div. front. Coys in trenches, dug outs etc on either side of RUE DE LA CHAPELLE 36/H.29 with Bn Hdqrs in CROIX MARECHAL.	
	11:10:18		C v D Coys moved nearer the front line occupying WHITE CITY POST 131 a v MOAT FARM AVENUE 125 a	
	14:10:18	2330	Unit relieved 36th Bn NORTH'D FUS. C v D Coys held posts on line running N v S through 36/I.34 a v C, v support platoons in INCUBATOR TR. v INCOME DRIVE 133 b v d A v B Coys in support in WHITE CITY POST 131 a v CITY POST H.36 d	
	15:10:18	1200.	On receipt of orders from Bde. General patrols from C v D coys sent out v found RADINGHAM RIDGE clear of enemy.	
		1600	C v D Coys moved forward to INDENT and INDEMNITY hand systems 135 with A v B Coys in close support in 134 a v C	
	16:10:18	0530	Artillery put down 30 minutes barrage on trenches I.36 and J.31. Barrage was very ineffective v often many shells fell short.	
		0600	C v D Coys moved forward to objective (trenches I.36 v J.31). There was considerable opposition from MGs in ditch in I.36 a v from FORT D'ENGLOS in P.1 a. They were engaged by Lewis Guns v Coys moved forward to objective	

WAR DIARY
or
INTELLIGENCE SUMMARY.
(Erase heading not required.)

Army Form C. 2118.

1st Royal Loch Fusiliers

Place	Date	Hour	Summary of Events and Information	Remarks and references to Appendices
36/1 36 v J 31.			A v B Coys then moved up to C v D's old line INDENT v INDEMNITY trenches. During the day there was a good deal of hostile shelling over the whole area as the result of which one of our patrols was wiped out. The weather was very bad v the men were exhausted. As we were out of touch with the Right Battn. A Coy provided a defensive flank.	
	17:10:18 0900.		Information was received that enemy had evacuated LILLE v its environments. A v B Coys moved forward with screen to LOMME v after a short rest to LA MADELEINE. The men had an enthusiastic welcome from the civilians reaching this place by 1500. One prisoner was captured in house in LOMME being the first to reach this place. Owing to verbal orders being received that unit had not to cross the HAUTE DEULE canal the Battn was withdrawn to the WEST side of the canal with posts on the EAST side.	
	18:10:18 0900		Battn moved forward A v B Coys leading with KING EDWARD'S HORSE v XI (BRDS CYCLISTS out as a screen. C v D were in close support. moving in march formation. There was some opposition from FORT MONS L 32 a v from house in L 33 d B 0.2 of these were cleared. Patrols pushed through ANNAPPES v then ASCQ v reported them clear of enemy. Battn moved forward to position in front of ASCQ at 1600.	
			There was hostile shelling (including gas) of FLERS, ANNAPPES v ASCQ during these operations.	
		1700.	Coys moved forward to its final objective for the day, in 37/M 8 a v C, 14 b v C. The units on right v left were 3000 - 4000 yards behind FORREST LILLE During the night a patrol entered FORREST LILLE v reported it all clear	

Army Form C. 2118.

WAR DIARY
or
INTELLIGENCE SUMMARY.
(Erase heading not required.)

1 Royal Scots Fusiliers

Place	Date	Hour	Summary of Events and Information	Remarks and references to Appendices
WILLEMS 37/M.6.12	19:10:18	07.30	Batn side stepped 1000* moved forward to its first objective WILLEMS (M.6 & M.12) The ground was practically all under water for 1st 1500*. But patrols went forward without hesitation & cleared up MG & Snipers posts. There was a great deal of hostile sniping during the whole of the day. A prisoner surrendered when Bn.Hr moved off-	
		10.00	Bn. reached WILLEMS (15 minutes after the enemy had evacuated it) The cavalry screen came in 30 minutes later. The left Batn owing to an error in their orders came along between same boundaries as ourselves but 2 hours behind us. The right Bn at 1000 had not started & was therefore 4000* behind us. This meant that defensive flanks had to be put out while Batn rested. Hereby causing more fatigue to the men than was necessary.	
TRIEU de WAZON 37/N.3.		15.30	Bn moved forward to its next objective & took up a position east of TRIEU de WAZON 37/N.3 arriving there after slight opposition at 17.00. A right defensive flank had to be thrown out-	
	20:11:18	16.00	Bn moved forward to HOUILLY. There was considerable hostile shelling of woods & roads. When HOUILLY was reached strong fighting patrols with MGs & sections from MGC was sent forward by C & D Coy (leading Coys) to search woods & buildings thus on west side of river ESCAUT. They reported ground clear of enemy & also that all bridges across the river destroyed. There was one small foot bridge but it had been drawn up on to the far bank.	
HOUILLY 37/N.5		14.00	C & D Coys moved up to 131.b.6.d. A & C Coys in close support in aerodrome 131.b.	

WAR DIARY
or
INTELLIGENCE SUMMARY. 11th Royal North Fusiliers

Army Form C. 2118.

Place	Date	Hour	Summary of Events and Information	Remarks and references to Appendices
PONT-A-CHIN 37/132;/26.	21.10.18	0930	A & B Coys moved up to effect crossing of the R. L'ESCAUT. B Coy (left Front Coy) moved to PONT-A-CHIN to ruined bridge. 2nd Lieut PATON with a strong telephone wire climbed over the ruins of the bridge & fastened wire to the footbridge 50x South of the ruined bridge. This party were eventually pulled into position & several men crossed. During these operations some Boche ran towards PARADIS firing a white Verey light. This brought heavy artillery fire on to PONT-A-CHIN. (There were indications also that some of the natives were signalling to the enemy for whenever a platoon was moved, it was shelled). A Coy (Right Front Coy) with C Coy immediately behind it moved along southern edge of CHATEAU de CHIN wood but owing to a concentration of machine fire from a cement-shewing the Red Cross v/from a signal cabin, v also of hostile shelling of all calibres the coys could not get to the river v eventually after having many casualties withdrew to its starting point. When B Coy heard of this withdrawal, v knowing that the left Bn.Hn was not going to attempt a crossing, it decided to leave a strong Lewis gun post to guard the bridge v withdraw the men from the heavily shelled village.	SS
		2020	Bn.Hn relieved by the 2/4 Bn. LOYAL NORTH LANCS 57 Divn. Unit marched back to N.W. outskirts of TEMPLEUVE yt 33a H25d v CROMBUE H25b.	
	22.10.18		From PLEUVE heavily shelled during night Bn.Hn moved to CHAOS H25d	SS

Army Form C. 2118.

WAR DIARY
or
INTELLIGENCE SUMMARY.
(Erase heading not required.)

11 Royal Scots Fusiliers

Instructions regarding War Diaries and Intelligence Summaries are contained in F.S. Regs, Part II. and the Staff Manual respectively. Title pages will be prepared in manuscript.

Place	Date	Hour	Summary of Events and Information	Remarks and references to Appendices
CHAOS	23/10/18		Battn standing by ready to move on half an hours notice to assist 177th Bde if River L'ESCAUT is crossed or to counter attack if necessary	
	24 "			
	25 "		Men having baths & occupied in repairing roads & craters in vicinity of their billets	
	26 "		Close order drill and Lewis Gun instruction	
	27 "		Officers Tactical classes & riding classes in afternoons	
	29 "			
	30 "			
	31	0900	Brigade Tactical Scheme. 11th R.S.F. on right front.	
		1300	STRENGTH OF BATTALION	

Arrivals

3/10/18. LT A.M. KENNEDY M.C. 3rd R.S.F
        LT J GRELLIS M.C. 5 Borders
10/10/18. 2/Lt W.K. PATON 3 R.S.F
          2/Lt W GORDON do
16/10/18 L' J DALZIEL S.R.S.F
          Capt D.C. BROWN Base
18/10/18 2/Lt N.J.GRAHAM from Bde Hdqrs
22/10/18 Capt C. NORBURY 7th Manch. Regt from 9th Corps Intell.
          Capt A.B. NAYLOR from Div School.

Departures

4 2/Lt W ABSOM UK Wounds   ⎫ Struck
7 Capt H CHRISTIE UK Sick   ⎬ off
14 Lieut DE RILEY B27 POW.   ⎭
                    AG 700/4836 (M) ⎫ strength
11 2/Lt FARRER AG 5416   ⎭
17 Capt PETTIGREW UK Spec leave
20 2/Lt N.J.GRAHAM L.G. School GHQ
24 Lt H.A. PRATT Hosp Sick
22 Capt D.C. BROWN Div. Recep Camp
24 2/Lt G.B. FLEMING 178 Bde
26 Capt A.F. TREMBER Hosp Sick
27 2/Lt W CONNELLY Wounded
27 Major A.L. MACMILLAN to assume command
28 Capt. QM D HIGHET 6 D.L.I. BTS
29 Lt J DALZIEL Div Recep Camp
30 2/Lt C.P. DALY Hosp Sick
31 Capt NORBURY 5th Army Inf School

Army Form C. 2118.

WAR DIARY
or
INTELLIGENCE SUMMARY.
(Erase heading not required.)

1/1 Royal Scots Fusiliers

Place	Date	Hour	Summary of Events and Information	Remarks and references to Appendices
			Strength of Battn continued —	
			Other Ranks	
			Arrivals	
			from Hosp 42	
			" Brigade 1	
			" Missing 1	
			Reinforcements 5	
			――	
			49	
			Departures	
			Sick 68	
			Wounded 37	
			Killed 10	
			Died of Wounds —	
			Missing b/w Killed 4	
			Missing b/w Killed 3	
			Corr Base Dept 3	
			AAG 3rd Army A/5/66 3	
			――	
			129	
			HONOURS. T/Lt (A/Capt) P. Dale; T/Lt(A/Capt) W. PETTEGREW; T/2/Lt(A/Capt T.H. OAKDEN DSO awarded the MILITARY CROSS	
			50592 Pte Saint H 51178 Pte Fletcher J 61965 Pte Barlow A) awarded the	
			207952 " Brocks J 265547 Sergt Thomson J P 266746 L/Cpl Mackenzie R W } MILITARY	
			59103 " McKinna R 266516 Pte Edgar A 59268 Pte Jeffreys W H MEDAL	
			PROMOTIONS etc T/Lt P DALE } to be capt whilst in command	
			T/2/Lt H OAKDEN DSO } of a company	
			LT J GRELLIS MC to be acting adjutant vice Capt L F TREMEER	
			[signature] Lieut Col.	
			Commdg 1/1 Bn Royal Scots Fusiliers	

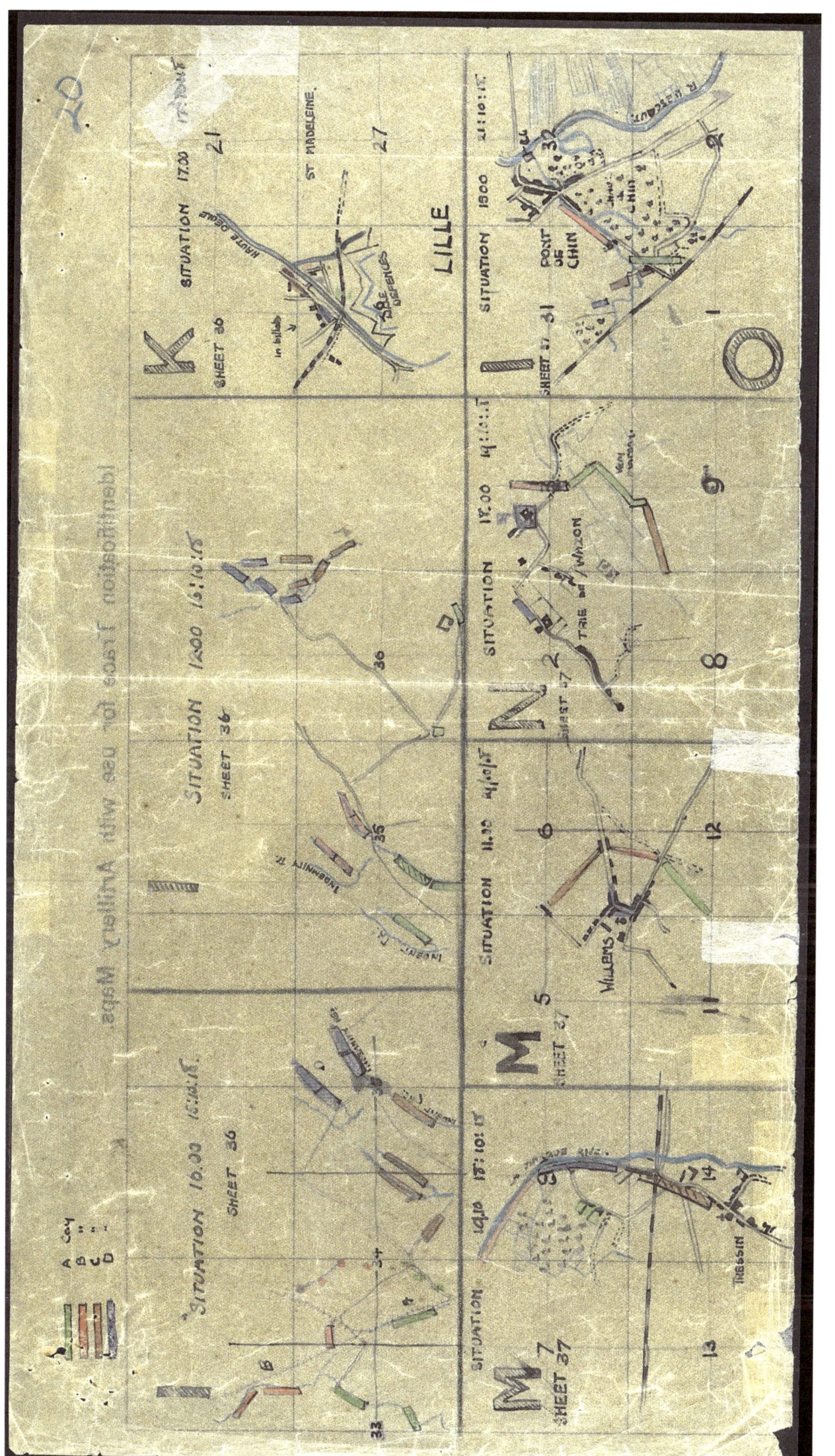

1.

(7) Copy of Operation order wired from JUGU
to PAQU   Sheet 36

"Right Boundary I 34 c 00 — I 35 c 0.0. — J 32 a 00
I 28 c 00 grid running eastwards to K 15 d 00
thence to K 26 b 0 6 — K 28 a 00 — cross roads
K 35 a 3.2. aaa"..... "Inter Battn Boundary
I 28 c 0.5. — I 30 c 05 — J 25 Cent — J 27 a 05
J 30 a 0.5 — Fork roads J 30 b 3.6. — thence along
roads NE to K 19 c 5.4 — K 20 cent — K 21 cent
— cross roads K 28 b 7.7 aaa

    First 3 bounds unaltered
4th Bound J 28 d 4.0 — J 28 d 4.6 along rd to J 21 b 90
5th -do-   railway from J 29 d 00 to J 23 b 8.1
6th -do-   road from J 30 d 90 — J 30 b 4.6. — North to CHATEAU
        in J 24 d
7th -do-   road N v S through K 20 cent.
8th -do-   road N v S through K 22 a.c v K 28 a.c

  14/10/18.

2.
Copy of SITUATION report of PAQU to JUGU
15.00   15/10/18

C Coy   right front Coy, posts in INDENT RES.
         " liaison post 36/1 36 c 15.40.
         2 Platoons in INDENT SWITCH.
         1 Platoon at Coy Hdqrs I 34 d 25.40
D Coy   left front Coy   Coy Hdqrs and –
         2 Platoons   INDEMNITY RES
         2 Platoons   — do —   SUPPORT
A Coy   right supp coy } in trenches & CTs in
B Coy   left supp Coy } I 34 a & c

——————— " ———————

~~Copy of SITUATION REPORT of PAQU to JUGU
1600   16:10:18~~

1/ Copy of Telegram from 178th Bde to this unit
BM 109.   15/10/18

" In order to co-operate with division on right the advance will commence at 0530 tomorrow aaa.

PAQU & PATI will advance & capture the main trench line J 31 Cent. J 25 c 00 J 19 d 00. J 19 Cent aaa

The artillery will put down a standing barrage on this line from 0530 to 0600 aaa

The Brigade on left will co-operate aaa "

JUGU b PAQU

Copy of Battn OPERATION ORDER
15/10/18

JUGU operation order. — In order to co-operate with div. on right, advance will commence at 0530. tomorrow aaa PAQU & PATI will advance & capture the main trench line J 31 Cent, J 25 c 00, J 19 d 00 J 19 Cent. Artillery will put down barrage on this line from 0530-0600 aaa Bde on left will co-operate.

Battn South Bdy J 31 Cent. North Bdy J 25 a 60. Inter Coy Bdy J 25 c 00. Coys will advance on a 2 Platoon front aaa A & B will move forward in rear & prepare to assist in counter-attack if necessary.

15/10/18   Signed L F Treneer
                        Capt & Adj.

Copy of to

Extract from letter from L'Col J.H. de la Perrelle Commanding 11th Bn R Sco Fus to 178th Bde

"---- There has been a great deal of shelling over the sector presumably owing to the movement on the roads. Battn Hdqrs receiving its share of attention.

Cannot get into touch with Battn on right. Battn officers and men did exceptionally well this morning, getting forward in spite of heavy Machine gun fire & sniping. They are however very tired, not having had any sleep on relief night or last night & especially having to be bustled off without breakfast. On going round this afternoon I found the men absolutely dead-beat

16/10/18

Signed J.H. de la Perrelle
L'Col Commanding
11th Bn R. Scot Fus

Copy of wire from JUGU to PAQU

" at 1700 today PATI & PAQU will halt aaa

Slight advances will be made will be made after dark to mislead enemy as to location of our line aaa

Touch must be established throughout Bde front & with units on flanks aaa

Hostile shelling of roads & localities may be expected tonight cover against shell fire must be constructed

1500
16/10/18.

Copy of Batt<u>n</u> OPERATION ORDER
F617 16.

At 0930 tomorrow A & B Coys will continue attack aaa Objective 3 Bound road running through J 26 d, J 32 c aaa Artillery barrage for 20 minutes from 0930 aaa

A & B Coy will move up into present front line before dawn aaa Boundaries Battn as marked on map aaa Inter Coy J 31 a 00 65 to J 25 d 75.20. thence to J 26 d 00.15 aaa C & D Coys will follow in support & will be prepared to strengthen attack or resist counter-attack aaa RAP at Battn HQ J 34 d 25.45 aaa. Report Centre at present D Coy Hdqrs J 30 d 75.45 aaa Advanced beaver post J 35 c 6.4.

0120

16/10/18

L F Tremeer
Capt & Adj

Copy of SITUATION REPORT to JUGU
20.00   17/10/18

Our present position is on West side of the HAUTE DEULE canal with outposts thrown out on the East side.

At 15.30 the battn were in the position given in divisional orders as the eighth objective (road running N v S in K 22 a & v c + K 28 a) with outposts thrown forward to the broad road K 28 b, d v c.

In accordance with verbal orders given by the Bde Commander to the CO of this unit, the battn was withdrawn to the outpost ~~line~~ position given in the first para.

Bn Hdqrs are at K 26 a 55.75

20.00   Signed L F Tremear
17/10/18   Capt v adj

Extracts from 178th Bde order No 145.
18/10/18.

① ----
②/ The advance will be resumed to-day
The K.E.H will move so as to be in
position by 0930 establishing posts at
L 25 c 5.3, L 19 a 1.0. and K 18 Central
   KEH Patrols will be pushed forward to
ascertain if the enemy are holding the line
ANNAPPES (R 9 v 10) L 27 – L 20 L 13 L 14
v the Canal L 1 c and d
③ 178th Bde will secure the inner line of the
LILLE defences on the east-side of the city
— on the general line of FLERS, — L 32 a, — L 28 a
Right Bdy   K 27 a 0.5 — K 34 c 6.4 — FLERS (incl)
Inter Battn Bdy   K 21 a 0.0 — Cross Rds K 28 d
      T roads K 30 a 0.0 — grid to L 27 c 0.0
④ The 11th RSF will establish posts east of FLERS
   + along road L 32 d 8.3 — L 27 c 1.1
⑤ Front line battns will be on road K 28 a K 22 b
   at 0930 + will advance at that hour.
⑥ Should the enemy have retreated the 11th RSF
v the 13 D of Ws will be prepared to move
forward in march formation under screen
of K E H
                     Signed H Trollope Ca/a
00.01   B M
18/10/18.   178th Inf Bde

Extract from BATTN OPERATION ORDER
F 627   17/10/18

C & D Coys will move forward tomorrow morning. A & B Coy will move in support a.a.a. C & D Coys will be on road running through K 28 c, K 28 a, K 22 c at 0830 ready to move. B Coy will be in support to D on Left, ready to move at 0830. a.a.a.

F 628   18/10/18
Right Bdy. K 27 a 05 – K 34 c 6.4 – FLERS (incl.)
Left Bdy.   K 21 a 00 – Cross roads K 28 b 77
            T roads K 30 d 00
Inter Coy Bdy. K 28 a 3.6 K 36 Central & Grid running East.

Coys will move forward at 0930 a.a.a. C & D Coys will establish posts East of road, FLERS – L 32 d 83 – L 27 c 11.

Should enemy have retreated Coys will be prepared to move forward by march route under screen of K.E.H. R.A.P at K 28 a 5.8 (Bn Hq). On reaching first objective Coys will report to Bn HQ. a.a.a. If advance continues reports to L 32 c 85.45. a.a.a.

S A A & L G amm. may if required be drawn from B HQ.

                                    Signed L F TREMEER
0230   Capt & adj
18/10/18

Copy of SITUATION REPORT of PAQU
to JUGU   19.10   18/10/18

Enemy in FOREST LILLE

'D' Coy holding W. bank of canal 37/M8d
  from M8b3.0 to M8d.3.1
'C' Coy holding road from M8d.3.1 to M14a8.0
  Liaison post with DEVONS (74th Div) at
  latter point
A Coy in support in M8c Central
B Coy have defensive flank from M7b8.8
  to M8b3.0

There is a gap of 1500x between the left
of the defensive flank & the foremost right
post of the Left Battn. Can this be
remedied as we are already out of
our boundary.

19.10   18/10/18.   Signed J Edward Robson
                                Lieut
                                Bn. I.O

Copy of Operation Orders of 178th Bde

① 178th Inf Bde will continue its advance today in conjunction with divisions on right & left.

② 57th div will advance astride the LILLE-TOURNAI railway & later fill gap between 74th Div & the Brigade.

Objectives allotted to 59th Division WILLEMS - SAILLY les LENNOY line. — TREU de WAZON - TEMPLEURE — HOLONS H21c

KEH will cross MARQUE at 0700

The Brigade will advance at 0800 & will make a further advance from first objective at 1300

36 NF will be in position W of BOIS D'ANMAPES at 0600 & will fill gap between 11th RSF & Bde on left by 0745

Right Bdy M 7 cent — N 7 cent — N 8 cent N 5 cent O 1 cent

Inter Battn Bdy M1 cent M 2 cent H 35 cent I 31 cent

0300
19/10/18

Signed — Trollope
Capt
Bde Maj
178th Inf Bde

Copy of SITUATION REPORT

18.00   19:10:18

Right Coy C   No 1 Post   N8d 2.4,   no 3 at N8b8.0
                2 "   N8d 7.5,   " 4 at N9c 8.8
                no 5 at N9c 9.4

Centre Coy A   No 1 Post N9b 2.4,   no 2 at N3d 2.2
                no 3 at N3d 5.5,   no 4 N3d 2.8

Left Coy B   3 posts on line N3b 0.7 —
               N3d 0.7
               Remainder at Coy Hdqrs N3a 6.3.

D Coy   in support   N2b.

18.00   Signed J. Edward Robson
                                      Lieut
19/10/18   Bn I.O

14

Copy of Wires from JUGU to PAQU.
BM-8   20/10/18
"Bde will advance to line of TOURNAI –
TURCOING railway 1000 yards & later will push
forward to R' ESCAUT with posts on eastern
bank. - - - - - "

BM 9.
In amplification of BM 8 Bde will effect
a crossing at PONT-A-CHIN & establish a
bridgehead. aaa PAFA - PAQU will advance at
10.00 to the general line N5b, N29d aaa PAQU will
be prepared to form a defensive flank facing BLANDAIN
aaa From this line each battn will send forward a
strong patrol supported by infantry & machine guns
to ascertain the enemy dispositions in the woods
lining the Western bank of the ESCAUT. aaa
Later PAFA will effect a crossing at PONT-A-CHIN
& PAQU will ascertain if there are any bridges on his
front aaa Pontoons cannot be used until the
situation is clearer. aaa K.E.H. are in div.
reserve
    Right Bde Bdy N 6 Central — O 6 · Cent
    Inter Bn Bdy. H 35 a 00 — I 35 a 00

    0815. 19/10/18

Copy of Wire from JUGU to PAQU.
BM 50   21

On the 21st the Bde in conjunction with 57th Div v 176th Bde will effect crossing of the ESCAUT v later gain the high ground in J 25 aaa PAFA v PAQU will cross the river & gain the line of the TOURNAI – HÆRINNES railway. by 10·00 aaa Artillery will put down a barrage at 0900 to rake from a line 400ˣ west of rly to the rly. & will fire as rapidly as the ammunition supply allows aaa from 0930 to 0945 no fire west of railway aaa 09·45 on road running through O 4 a, 134 c & a and 127 d aaa C/QENO will thicken up artillery barrage with MG barrage NOT to fire west of railway, to lift from railway at 0930 aaa

Crossings will be effected at O 3 c 3.4 – PONT A CHIN and 126 c aaa The necessary reconnaissance of these points will be carried out aaa At 1200 PAFA will advance to road 134 a v 127 d aaa PAQU will form a defensive flank at 134 a 4.0 back to river in O 2 b aaa From this line PAFA will move forward & establish posts about 134 cent – 134 b 07 – 128 d 03 aaa Rt Bde Bdy O 1 cent to O 6 cent Later Bn Bdy 1 32 cent to J 31 cent .. . . .

Instructions for capture of high ground in J 19 v 25 follow.

0430
21/10/18

Copy of Wire from JUGU to PAQU
SM 51   21

Capture of high ground in J 25 will be carried out by PAFA in conjunction with 176th Bde who will occupy J 19 in accordance with following instructions aaa

General line of advance will be approx. along the right div. Bdy aaa Bde on left moving along left Div. boundary As PAFA advances detachments will turn inwards & press up the southern spurs of MONT ST AUBERT J 28 & 29 & 30. aaa   Posts will be established on the low ground to sweep the re-entrants & cover the movement of these detachments on to the high ground aaa

It is essential that posts & detachments give mutual supporting fire to each other aaa as PAFA advances, PAQU will form a defensive flank from J 36 central to KAIN inclusive in O & b aaa

The actual time for these operations wel will be notified later

05.45

21/10/18

Copy of Battn Operation Orders

A & B Coys will effect crossing of river & gain line of TOURNAI – HERINNES rly by 10.00 today. C & D Coys will search for barrels, boards & other materials to make temp. bridge & will cross afterwards. At 12.00 PAFA will advance to line of road I34 a I27 d. This unit will form strong defensive flank from I34 a 4·0 to river in O2b. B Coy from I34 a 4·0 to rly. A Coy from rly (incl) to I33 d to I33 c 8·0. C Coy from I33 c 8·0 to river in O2b. D Coy in support in I33c. Barrage will be put down at 0900 to rake from 400ˣ W of railway to Rly. From 0930 to 0945 no fire W of rly. At 0945 on road running through O4a, I34 c and a. and I27 d.

Later high ground in J25 will be carried by PAFA. General line of advance will be along Right Div'n Bdy. As PAFA advances detachments will turn inwards and press up Southern spurs of MONT ST AUBERT I28, 29 I30. PAQU will form defensive flanks from I36 Cent to KAIN (incl) in O4b. Coys will move on to this second defensive flank from first in same order.

Actual time of advance will be notified later. Rations to be carried on man.

Acknowledge

Sign. L F Tremeer
Capt & Adj.

0830

21/10/18

Copy of SITUATION REPORT of PAQU

1400   21/10/18

B Left Front Coy proceeded to PONT/A/CHIN. An officer crossed the ruins of the old bridge with a line (telephone wire). He fastened this to the swing foot pontoon bridge that had been pulled across by the Bosche on retiring. The bridge was then pulled into position. As this was being done, 2 enemy ran towards BARADIS one of them firing a white Verey light

A Right Front Coy approached the canal by the southern edge of the CHAU de CHIN wood followed by C. Coy. They came under very heavy M.G. fire from the convent O.2.d. v the signal cabin O.3.b.5.7. v Artillery fire from the Southern slopes of MONT. ST. AUBERT. They were unable to get forward v had to withdraw after having fairly heavy casualties

B on receipt of this information v knowing that the Left Battn was not attempting to cross, did not cross the canal.

Dispositions at present
A Coy. I.31.d.5.1. to Railway crossing O.1.b. cent.
B Coy. L.G. post watching PONT. A. CHIN bridge
    v defensive line from X roads I.33.c.4.5
    I.31.d.5.1.
C in support I.31.d.0.7
D "   "   I.31.d.4.3
                                    Signed J Edward Robson
1500.
21/10/18.   Bn IO

Copy of wire from JUGU to PAQU
BM 69.   21/10/18

JUGU will be relieved to night by Bde of 57 div. aaa
On completion of relief the Bde will be disposed as follows aaa
PAQU H 25 b . . . . . aaa
Bde Hdqrs to CHAOS H 30 Central aaa
Completion of relief to be reported to TEMPLEUVE CHAU. aaa

17.55

21/10/18

0815 -19/10/18 should read 0815 20/10/18. This message is B.M.9 and the previous one B.M 8 (at top of this page) is dated 20/10/18. See also diary of 3/N.F (178 Bde) for 20/10/18.

WAR DIARY
INTELLIGENCE SUMMARY

11th R. Scots Fusiliers — Army Form C. 2118.

November 1918.

Place	Date	Hour	Summary of Events and Information	Remarks and references to Appendices
CHAOS ~ FORZEAU H.25 c/d Sheet 36	Nov 1, 2, 3, 4, 5, 6, 7		178th Bde in Divisional Support. Battn in billets carrying out ordinary training & instruction. Unit ready to move on half an hours notice to assist 177th Bde in capturing MONT DE LA TRINITE if attack be made.	
	1st	0730	GOC 59th Division presented ribbons of Military Cross to — Capt TH OAKDEN OBO and Capt RD DALE. Ribbons for the Military Medal were presented to:— 6/11575 Pte Fletcher J 265547 Sgt Thompson JP 266516 Pte Edgar A S/10665 " Barton AJ 266640 L/Cpl McKenzie RM 59368 " Jeffreys WH 201452 " Brooks J 59103 Pte McKinnon R	
	7		Battn relieved 2/6th Bn DURHAM LIGHT INFANTRY on posts on West bank of River L'ESCAUT (Scheldt) relief complete by 19.30 hours. Very quiet night, one hostile M.G. fired until 23.30 nothing afterwards.	
	9	0730	Bhqs crossed the river & could find no trace of the enemy. Battn moved forward C v D leading with A + B in support. The KING EDWARD'S HORSE moved through as no opposition whatever.	
		1100	RUET DU SART reached. 3 ammn MG wappons of enemy found on road forming a screen. Battn rested for 2 hours.	

Army Form C. 2118.

WAR DIARY
or
INTELLIGENCE SUMMARY.
(Erase heading not required.)

Instructions regarding War Diaries and Intelligence Summaries are contained in F. S. Regs., Part II. and the Staff Manual respectively. Title Pages will be prepared in manuscript.

Place	Date	Hour	Summary of Events and Information	Remarks and references to Appendices
	Nov. 9.	1330	Battn moved on to its final Objective VELAINES arriving there about 1500. a german army major dressed in civilian clothes was taken at his village. Outpost line thrown out 1500 × east of VELAINES	1
	10th		Advance resumed There was no opposition whatever N high ground North of FRASNES-LEZ-BUISSENAL was reached by 1300. Outpost line established on east easy spurs in 37/L4 v 10. This Division (50th) tarshand fast step. 74th Div pass through it	
	11.	1100	Cessation of Hostilities. Battn remained in positions of previous night During afternoon 74th Div passed through to took up a Line 1977-LESSINES	
	12.	1400	Battn marched back to VELAINES about 6 miles	
VELAINES 37/K 13	13. 14. }		Battn resting at VELAINES cleaning up etc. Battn inspected by B.G.C. 177th Inf Bde & highly praised for the work of the last few months.	
PECQ 37/I.1.	15.		Battn marched from VELAINES to PECQ about 9 miles One hour half at RUST DU SART for hot dinners. No one fall out	
WILLEMS 37/M 5.	16.		Battn moved from PECQ to WILLEMS 6½ miles Conditions ideal for marching fine and frosty	
PT RONCHIN 36/G 22.	17.		Battn moved from WILLEMS to PT RONCHIN. 10-11 miles one hour halt for hot dinners.	
	18 to		Battn in billets in PETITE RONCHIN One hour per day military training Each afternoon spent in organised sports.	

ically Form C. 2118.

WAR DIARY
or
INTELLIGENCE SUMMARY.
(Erase heading not required.)

Place	Date	Hour	Summary of Events and Information	Remarks and references to Appendices
PETITE RONCHIN M 36/A 22	23rd		Men classified under new Educational Scheme.	
	24th		Batt route march. LESQUIN - MERCHIN - GRANDE RONCHIN 6 miles	
	26		Brigade united Thanksgiving Service to Church of England	
			17th Brigade inspected by GOC 59th Division who presented ribbons to the officers	
			NCOs & men who had been awarded decorations.	
			Capt. W. PETTIGREW received ribbon of the Military Cross.	
			The following NCOs & men of his unit received ribbons of the Military Medal.	
			2616640 SGT. FURST. 265437 SGT McGREGOR J. 266463 CORPL BLACK J	
			53972 L/CPL LIVINGSTONE W. 266295 PTE SLOAN F.H. 59725 PTE BLACK H.L.P	
			59622 PTE WELSH J	
	28th		This day (Thursday) was to have been a complete holiday but the Divisional Baths	
			(WATTIGNIES) were allotted to the Bon. for the day.	
			LT. COL. V.N. DE LA PERRELLE D.S.O. M.C. resumed command of the Bon from MAJOR	
			R.F.H. DICKS on return from leave.	
	30th		A Coy won the Soccer match (Semi-Final) Bon Bde Cup vs. Bde H.Q. Score 4 v. 2	
			During the week two hours of each forenoon were devoted to military training and	
			in the afternoon an organised programme of sports was carried out under coy arrange-	
			ments.	
			Word was received that the move to the neighbourhood of BRUAY (1:40000 44B/S)	
			to which an advanced billeting party was sent on the 28th, was cancelled and	
			that the 17th Inf Bde was to proceed to DUNKIRK on detachment. An order was	
			dispatched recalling the advanced party	

Army Form C. 2118.

WAR DIARY
INTELLIGENCE SUMMARY.
(Erase heading not required.)

Instructions regarding War Diaries and Intelligence Summaries are contained in F. S. Regs., Part II. and the Staff Manual respectively. Title pages will be prepared in manuscript.

Place	Date	Hour	Summary of Events and Information	Remarks and references to Appendices
			Alteration of Strength during month.	
			(A) Officers.	
			(i) Increase:—	
	7/11/18		2/Lt W. Connelly "A" Return on Strength from Hospital.	
	11/11/18		Capt R.E.H. Dicks H.R Rfy. Bus. "A". Joined Bn. and assumes duty as Sec. in Cmd.	
			2/Lt G. Green W. Yorks Regt "A" Joined Bn.	
	18/11/18		Lt R. Strong M.C. Border Regt "A" Joined Bn.	
	" "		Lt B. Pitt Lovats Scouts "C" do	
	19/11/18		2o 9 2nd Lt F.T. Cooper "D" do	
			& assumes duty as 2/Lt	
	27/11/18		2/Lt A.J. Graham "B" Rejoined Bn. from leave. Reposted to "B" Coy.	
	29/11/18		2/Lt Col de la Perrelle "A" " " " "	
			total 8.	
			(ii) Decrease:—	
	1/11/18		2/Lt A.J.D Colsons "B" Proceeded to Special warfare course for Snipers at 5th Army Sgs. school, PREURES.	
	" "		2/Lt N.C. Donaldson "A" Granted Special leave to U.K. 3/11/18 - 17/11/18 via Calais	
	3/11/18		Capt A.B. Naylor "A" Proceeded to H.Q 59th Div. for duty w. Q. Branch.	
	4/11/18		2/Lt D. w. m. Mathison "C" Proceeded on leave 4/11/18 - 20/11/18, via Calais.	
	7/11/18		Capt. & Q.M. D. Hughes Struck off strength on proceeding to U.K. and, A.G.	
			2158/7345. (O.)	

WAR DIARY

INTELLIGENCE SUMMARY.

(Erase heading not required.)

Army Form C. 2118.

Place	Date	Hour	Summary of Events and Information	Remarks and references to Appendices
	13/11/18		**Alterations & Strength during month (cont:)** — A. Officers. (ii) Decrease. (cont.) Capt. C. Norbury "A" Struck off strength on posting to 1/7th Bn Manchester Regt. Auth: A.G. 2158/6427 (O) d. 29/10/18	
	" "		2/Lt. H.J. Graham "B" Ordinary Leave to U.K. to 24/11/18 via Calais Lt Col. J.N. de la Perrelle D.S.O, M.C., "A" proceeded on Leave to U.K. 13/11/18 to 26/11/18 via Calais.	
	22/11/18		Capt. R. Bate M.C. "C" do Leave. 22/11/18 Lt R.T. Vaughan "D" " " "	
	22/11/18		2/Lt W. Gordon "D" do course 1st Army musketry comt.	
	27/11/18		Lt. J.R. Rotton "B" Leave to U.K. 26/11/18 2/Lt P.C.S. Smith "B" do. Total 13.	
			B. Other Ranks. (i) Increase :- Reinforcements 27 From E.E.S. etc hospitals 15 Army Command Schools 21 From Leave. 3 ___ Total :- 66	

WAR DIARY
INTELLIGENCE SUMMARY.
(Erase heading not required.)

Army Form C. 2118.

Place	Date	Hour	Summary of Events and Information	Remarks and references to Appendices
	1.12.18.		Alteration of Strength (contd.) Both Ranks. (contd.). (ii) Decrease. Killed and wounded . . . . nil Sick to Hospitals . . . . 35 Leave to U.K. . . . . 9 To courses . . . . 21 To Base or other units . . . . 9 Total 74	Alex J. B. Porteous 2/Lt. for Lt. Col. Comdg. 2nd Bn. J. O. Scots Fus.

S E C R E T

Addendum No. 4. to
178th Infantry Brigade Order No. 145.

4th Nov. 1918.

FURTHER INSTRUCTIONS FOR THE CAPTURE
OF MONT ST. AUBERT AND MONT DE LA TRINITE.
----

1. (a) This operation would be carried out in conjunction with the Divisions on our Right and Left.

   (b) The Division on our right is to advance between the RIVER MELLES AND MONT ST. AUBERT to capture the spur in J.25.d. and b.
   Their immediate objectives are to be –

   1st – TOURNAI – HERINNES railway.
   2nd – LA TOMBE (O.11.a.) – Buildings in O.5.c. – KAIN (O.5.b.) – I.28.Central.

   From the Second objective their left brigade is to send out strong patrols to reconnoitre the Southern slopes of MONT ST. AUBERT with a view to attacking MONT ST. AUBERT from the SOUTH WEST.

   (c) The Division on our left is to gain the spur I.11.Central – I.6.Central – D.15.Central.

2. Forty-eight hours' notice will be given before the Division is required to effect the capture of MONT DE LA TRINITE in the face of strong enemy opposition.

   This notice will not apply in case of enemy weakening.

3. The essentials for success are surprise and rapidity of execution. Therefore –

   (a) There will be no preliminary bombardment.
   (b) The attacking troops will be assembled on the Eastern bank of the river L'ESCAUT under cover of darkness, and will advance at Zero Hour.

4. The advance to the first objective will be carried out under cover of a heavy "crash" bombardment to be arranged by the C.R.A., and supported by the fire of machine guns, which will be co-ordinated by the O.C., Machine Gun Battalion, Lewis Guns and Light Trench Mortars pushed forward into the marshes will engage known enemy posts at Zero.
   At Zero hour, the Heavy Artillery is to neutralise all known hostile batteries which can bring fire to bear on our advanced troops.

5. On the capture of the Second Objective touch must be established with the Division on our right about I.28.c.5.7. (road junction).

6. After the capture of MONT DE LA TRINITE, 177th Infantry Brigade by a further turning movement from the North will establish posts on the line J.19.d.5.0. – REJET DU SART (J.20.c.) – Chapel (J.14.d) – and gain touch with the Division on our right about J.19.d.5.0.

7. The policy of the employment of Mounted Troops is as follows:-

P.T.O.

(a) The Corps Mounted Troops will assemble about H.23.c. and H.20.b. & d., and on the 177th Infantry Brigade reaching the line J.19.d.5.0. - REJET DU SART - Chapel (J.14.d.) Corps Mounted Troops will then move via MOURCOURT (J.28.c.) towards MELLES (J.36.b.). After passing through 177th Inf.Bde. XI Corps Mounted Troops will come under the orders of G.O.C. Division on our right.

(b) The advanced troops of the 177th Inf.Bde. in position on the spurs about REJET DU SART will be prepared to support this movement by M.G. and rifle fire.

8. Further instructions will be issued on the following points:-

    (a) Artillery Barrage.
    (b) The details of the gas bombardment of MONT ST. AUBERT and MONT DE LA TRINITE.
    (c) Machine Gun Barrage.

9. Acknowledge.

(sgd) H. Trollope. Capt.
Brigade Major.
178th Infantry Brigade.

S E C R E T

Copy of **178th Infantry Brigade Advance Instructions No.I.**

Ref. Map Sheet 37, 1/40,000.   6th November, 1918.

178th Inf. Bde. Order No.145 is cancelled with the exception of the March Table and Addendum No.4, the latter being renumbered Instructions No.II.

1. The capture of MONT DE LA TRINITE will be carried out by the 177th Infantry Brigade, supported by 178th Infantry Brigade, and 176th Infantry Brigade will be in Divisional Reserve.

2. 177th Infantry Brigade will advance by bounds :-

   First Objective - TOURNAI - HERIHNES Railway.
   Second Objective - HAVRON - ORGIES road to I.9.d.1.1. thence along railway to Northern Boundary.
   From this objective strong patrols will move forward and establish posts about I.28.a.3.3., I.22.c.9.6., I.22.b.4.1., I.16.d.3.0., I.16.c.5.3., I.16.a.0.7., I.9.d.0.7., and a strong defensive flank will be thrown back towards the river.

3. After the capture of the Second Objective the 177th Infantry Brigade will advance along the general line of the LEAUCOURT - GOUDENIERE road and occupy MONT DE LA TRINITE and take up the final line J.19.d.5.0. - REJET DU SART.

4. As the 177th Infantry Brigade moves forward to its final objective 178th Infantry Brigade will take over the second objective laid down in para. 2 with 11th Royal Scots Fusiliers on the right and the 13th Duke of Wellington's on the left each finding their own supports, and the 36th Northumberland Fusiliers in Brigade Reserve in Squares I.19.c. & a, and I.13.c. & a.
   The 11th R.S.F. and 13th D. of W. are responsible for protecting the right and left flanks respectively of the 177th Infantry Brigade in the event of the Divisions on either flank being unable to cross the river.

5. Right Brigade Boundary. I.27.Central - I.22.d.0.0. grid line Eastwards to J.23.c.5.0. thence a line to K.20.Central.
   Left Brigade Boundary. I.8.Central through GRAND REJET and CLIPET both inclusive.
   Inter-Bn. Boundary.   I.14.d.0.0. - I.17.a.0.0. thence along grid line Eastwards to J.18.a.0.0. to K.7.c.0.0.

6. After the 177th Infantry Brigade has captured its final objective, the 178th Infantry Brigade, moving through the 177th Infantry Brigade, will advance by bounds :-

   1st Bound. Spur running N.N.E. from LA GRANDE BARAQUENNE through BOURGOYNE to CLIPET.
   2nd Bound. Road K.19.c.0.5. - East of VELAINES - CHAPEL J.12.d along road N.W. to FERME DU GRAND RUE RIEU

   36th Northumberland Fusiliers will move off at the same hour at the 11th R.S.F. and 13th D.of W. along the Main Divisional road and will keep from 3000 - 4000 yards in rear of the leading troops.

7. The order to move will be sent by telegraphing the word "MOVE" followed by zero hour, e.g., MOVE 1430.
   On receipt of this order Battalions will move in accordance with the March Table issued on October 26th which will be amended as follows :- The destination of Serial No.3 11th R.S.F. will read "2nd Objective".

-2-

8. 178th L.T.M.B. will move along the main Divisional Road close behind the leading troops, and each leading battalion will have a call on two guns if they are meeting with any resistance.

9. The Machine Gun Company attached to the Brigade will move off from their billets at zero plus 50 and will move by route in serial 2 of the March Table. When the Brigade passes through 177th Infantry Brigade one section will be attached to each leading battalion; the remainder of the Company will remain in Brigade Reserve and will move in rear of the 36th N.F.

10. Para.7 of Addendum No.4 is cancelled and the following substituted:-
The Corps Mounted Troops will remain under the orders of G.O.C. 59th Division after passing through the 177th Inf.Bde. and will ascertain whether the enemy is holding:-

   (a) The general line QUIEVREMONT J.22 - OLIPET J.10 both inclusive.
   (b) VELAINES and BERLION.

11. The Brigade will be ready to move at half an hour's notice.

12. Battalions will take transport laid down in para.1 of this Office letter 1113/6 of Oct. 23rd.
In the event of the bridges not being complete over the ESCAUT transport will be parked off the road.

13. Main Divisional Road runs as follows :-

   HEM
   SAILLY-LEZ-LANNOY
   TOUFFLERS
   NECHIN
   Road Junction H.10.d.25.45.
   BAILLEUL
   LE BUVRIERE FM. H.18.d.4.0.
   PAS A WASMES.
   Road Junction I.7.d.7.8.
   Road Junction I.13.d.8.9.
   Road Junction I.14.c.25.50.
   Main Bridge I.14.b.6.3.
   East Side of Canal to I.8.d.8.5.
   CABARET LIETARD.
   Road Junction I.17.c.7.4.
   Road Junction I.24.a.9.6.
   J.21.c.3.2.

14. Brigade H.Q. will remain in their present location and will move to ESQUELMES when vacated by 177th Inf. Bde. When the Brigade moves through the 177th Inf. Bde., Brigade H.Q. will open at the cross roads I.24.a.9.6., and finally move to FAUCHY J.22.c.1.3.

15. Acknowledge.

                        (Sgd) A.H. Trollope, Capt.
                            Brigade Major,
Issued at 1600.   178th Infantry Brigade.

Copy of Operation Orders of 178th Bde
10/11/18   BM 35

The advance will be continued to-day aaa First objective FOREST-CHAUNY, 2nd objective crossings over stream K.23.b Cent to L.1a cent aaa 3rd objective high ground L.4 and L.10 aaa Corps mounted troops will move through infantry outpost line at 0700 and will ascertain whether enemy is holding these objectives aaa At 0800 Bde will advance with 11th R.S.F on right and 13 D of W. on left. 36 NF in reserve aaa

Infantry will follow in rear of mounted troops & at dusk will take over positions of most advanced mounted troops. aaa On relief K.E.H will move back into billets aaa 2nd Hampshires && Regt Bde will be on left & 142nd Inf Bde will be on right aaa Right Boundary K 23 cent to L 16 cent aaa Left Boundary CHAUNY E 28 c — GRANQUIER F 30d aaa

Bde HQ will open at LA LAIE K7d at 0900 moving later to FERME DU CHATEAU K4d & finally to X roads K6d Cent. aaa 36th NF will move off at 0730 & keep 3000 - 4000 yards in rear of leading troops

                                Signed H W TROLLOPE
OO. O1   Capt Bde Major
10/11/18   178th Inf Bde

Copy of WIRE from JUGU to PAQU
BM1 9

PATI now at GRAND RESET in touch with 40th DIV. aaa.
GOC wishes you to push forward without stopping to VELAINES aaa
Bde Hqrs will be established for night at BOURGOYNE aaa KEH are now moving through

Copy of WIRE from JUGU to PAQU
   BM 1.   11.

Hostilities cease - 11.00 to day aaa
Brigade will not move to day aaa
no communication is to be held with the enemy
_____

Copy of WIRE from JUGU to PAQU.
   BM 2   11

In confirmation of BM1 aaa Hostilities will cease
1100 to day aaa Troops will stand fast in present
position aaa Battns will hold outpost line
until units of 74th Div have established a
line further east & are in front of them aaa
Touch will be gained with flank formations aaa
Line to be reported to Brigade HQ aaa
Precautions will be preserved and no
communication will be held with the enemy

   13·15 hours
      11/11/18.

11th. ROYAL SCOTS FUS.   DECEMBER 1918.

11/R.S.F.

December 1918.

WAR DIARY
or
INTELLIGENCE SUMMARY.

Army Form C. 2118.

Place	Date	Hour	Summary of Events and Information	Remarks and references to Appendices

PETIT RONCHIN
Sheet 36/Q22.

DEC.
1/12/18
to
3/12/18

The Battn. remained here under orders to move, first to DUNKIRK then by stages to BRUAY (Sheet 44 B/8). The usual programme was carried out & the forenoon aside organised sports by Coys in the afternoon military training.

2/12/18 11.00 Return of Advance Party recalled from BRUAY.
3/12/18 0700 The transport of the Bn. under Capt. Still set off by road to DUNKIRK with the remainder of 178th Bde. Transport. On relieving party under Lieut. A.M. Kennedy remained for recall from limits of 61st Divl. Area accepted at HAZEBROUCK when cycle were received.

1800 A Pack Concert was held organised by Capt. G.T. Wright C.F.
2100 Return of DUNKIRK Billeting Party.

4/12/18 0800 The 178th Bde entrained at PETIT RONCHIN for BRUAY where they arrived about
to 1300 1300 and marched to Co. camp (44B/V16d+P). The men were accommodated
13.30 in huts.
On the journey the 11th R.S.F. was the leading Battn. of the Bde. The route followed was via WATTIGNIES, SECLIN, CAMPHIN, CARVIN, LENS, LOOS, VERMELLES, NOEULLES, SAILLY LABOURSE, BETHUNE, FOUQUIERES, HAISDIGNEUL, LABUISSIERE. (Rd. 1:100000 TOURNAI 5/HAZEBROUCK 5A/LENS 11/HAZEBROUCK 5A/LANG 11.) The distance marched from DUNKIRK was mentioned at HAZEBROUCK 6.22.

BRUAY 5/12/18 The Battn. was at BRUAY and the usual programme of training and sports
(44B/V16d) 7 days was carried out.
to 6/12/18

The officers of the 11th R.S.F. entertained the G.O.C. 178 Bde and Staff to dinner in BRUAY.

Army Form C. 2118.

WAR DIARY
or
INTELLIGENCE SUMMARY.
(Erase heading not required.)

Instructions regarding War Diaries and Intelligence Summaries are contained in F. S. Regs., Part II. and the Staff Manual respectively. Title pages will be prepared in manuscript.

Place	Date	Hour	Summary of Events and Information	Remarks and references to Appendices
BRUAY (M.B./16) (1222.d.)	6.7.18		Lt/Col. J.A. de la Panouse DSO one temporarily assumed command of 174th Bde. during absence of Bt/G.O.C. at Dunkirk. Major R.E.H. Dick's assuming command of the Battn. (and command at Dunkirk 9/7/18). A Whist drive for the Battn. was organised by Capt. G.T. Wright OP.	
HOUVIN ECOUST (M.B./10)	8.7.18	2.PM to 6AM	The Battn. less "B" & "D" Coys was under the command of Major R.E.H. Dick's and marched via Divion & Camblain Châtelain to Calonne Ricouart (M.B./10) to entrain for Dunkirk via Bethune & Hazebrouck the loading parties for the transport of the advance parties to the Bde. The train due to depart at 1500 did not arrive till 1830 & left at 2200.	MAJOR H.K. HUGHES LANS 7/7/18 was put under the command of Capt. J.W. de la Panouse DSO MC
DUNKIRK (Maps Shelf 19/10)	9.7.18	0500 1000	Bde. advanced party arrived at Dunkirk Stn. (Lock wiring) where they de-trained and were taken to the "Citadel" where they breakfasted. (1922.85.45) the site of the former camp, tents & materials were drawn from Ordnance dumps and Camp was pitched up to 30. Autumn thrown were drawn by truck and munition stores.	MICHEL where we live conference after conference May 1918.
19B25D (M.B./10)	10.7.18	5pm	They were again recovered in erecting sufficient tents to accommodate the whole Bn. HQ were erected and the lines duckboarded. The weather was very wet. B.O. coys left Bruay by the first train and entrained at Dunkirk at 730. They were met by guides and marched to Camp arriving about 1030. Autumn transport was on arrival met by Capt. 5. While Bn. was in camp by 0300 1930	

D.D. & L., London, E.C. (A10266) Wt W5300/P713 750,000 2/15 Sch. 82 Forms/C2118/16

Place: DUNNIKIER 19/12/15

Date	Hour	Summary of Events and Information
12/12/15		Organisation of the Bn. for administrative purposes was inaugurated. A and B coys - "A" wing commanded by Col. W. Pettigrew. C and D coys - "B" wing " " Major R.E.H. Dare.
13/12/15		The Bn. was engaged in drawing materials for and erecting 300 tents, in A wing camp. Both in A wing went into tents and not hutments as first. C and D coys Erection of huts until more huts arrived to the first portion of huts. More huts are to be accommodated by A wing, various times during the day and more accommodation by A wing (approx 2000)
14/12/15		Work in B wing camp continued. More huts erected and more accommodation by A wing.
15/12/15		To end of the month, men arriving in both wings every 10 days for final sorting out of papers and equipment into drafts, the following are the members arriving and departing.
		A wing Arrivals 15 ors
12/12/15		- do - 39 officers 1705 ors
13/12/15		- do - 10 - 190 ors
14/12/15		- do - 3 - 190 ors
15-16		B Wing do 62 off 2791 ors embarked 16th inst and 18th inst
16		A Wing Embarkation 37 off 1954 ors To other camps, Hospital etc 21 OR
17,18		A Wing Arrivals 53 off 1624 ors
19		A Wing Embarkation 53 off 1621 ors To Hosp etc 3 ors
19-20		B Wing Arrivals 48 off 2264 ors
21		- do - 15 off 777 ors

Army Form C. 2118.

WAR DIARY
or
INTELLIGENCE SUMMARY.
(Erase heading not required.)

Instructions regarding War Diaries and Intelligence Summaries are contained in F. S. Regs., Part II. and the Staff Manual respectively. Title pages will be prepared in manuscript.

Place	Date	Hour	Summary of Events and Information	Remarks and references to Appendices
DUNKIRK	21/12/14		B Wing departures 28 officers 1457 OR A Wing Arrivals 7 off 355 OR	
Hospice S Pd	22"		- do - 15 off do 14 off 986 OR	
Camp	23		B Wing arrival 6 OR 777 OR	
(Rendolizaton)	24		A Wing departures 24 off 1340 OR	
			Men of 1st RSF and 178th T.M.B entertained to Christmas dinner. This was left	
			on this day in view of the fact that all the men would be employed on Xmas day	
	25"		B Wing departures 6 ors A Wing arrivals 57 off 2596 ors	
	26"		Officers of unit with Bde staff as guests, held their Xmas dinner at night.	
			New Zealand, Battn. 28 off 719 ors accomodated in 'B' Wing. They were unable to	
			embark until arrival of their transport personnel.	
			A Wing departures 12 off 600 ors	
	27-28		B Wing -do- New Zealand Battn. transferred to A Wing	
			B Wing arrivals 2266 ors A Wing 816 ors.	
	28"		A Wing departures 27 off 1201 ors B Wing 6 off 300 ors	
	29"		A Wing -do- 16 off 816 OR B Wing 42 off 1966 ors.	
			Camps particularly A Wing in disgraceful condition. The ground is very low lying with the	
			result that water is standing in many places. Many of the tents are under water.	

Army Form C. 2118.

WAR DIARY
or
INTELLIGENCE SUMMARY.
(Erase heading not required.)

Instructions regarding War Diaries and Intelligence Summaries are contained in F. S. Regs., Part II. and the Staff Manual respectively. Title pages will be prepared in manuscript.

Place	Date	Hour	Summary of Events and Information	Remarks and references to Appendices
DUNKIRK				
Hospice			Owing to the very bad state of the parade ground & approaches to the huts the men ate	
St Pol			drive in the camp made to give way to the dispersal stations on somewhat similar lines.	
Camp			Influenza epidemic among the New Zealand contingent & A Wing therefore	
(Demobilization)			placed out of bounds.	
	30/1/19		B Wing arrivals 35 officers 1582 ORs	
	31/1/19		— do — 23 officers 1254 ORs	
			INCREASE in PERMANENT STAFF during the month DECREASE	
			Officers	
			2nd Lieut C. Gordon—Cleather R Sussex Regt Capt DC Brown to BERGUES	
			Lieut P Bolton E Yorks Regt as Town Major	
			A/Lieut G R Flemmy from 178th Bde HQ	
			A Lieut RC Henderson 1st appointment	
			do C Godd do	
			do " TH Fedgate do	
			do TOR Farrow do	
			do W Goldstein do	

Army Form C. 2118.

WAR DIARY
or
INTELLIGENCE SUMMARY.
(Erase heading not required.)

Instructions regarding War Diaries and Intelligence Summaries are contained in F. S. Regs., Part II. and the Staff Manual respectively. Title pages will be prepared in manuscript.

Place	Date	Hour	Summary of Events and Information	Remarks and references to Appendices
			INCREASE (continued)	
			Other ranks	
			Reinforcements 10	
			From hospital 22	
			From Command 19	
			Total 57	
			DECREASE	
			To Hospital 34	
			To Home Establishment 5	
			To Command 10	
			To Base 4	
			Demobilisation – Miners 18	
			Total 71	

Aidela Orselle Lt Colonel
Com'dg 11. Royal Fusiliers
Jan 17. 1919

WAR DIARY

11th Bn. Royal Scots Fusiliers

January 1919.

INTELLIGENCE SUMMARY.

(Erase heading not required.)

Place	Date	Hour	Summary of Events and Information	Remarks and references to Appendices
DUNKERQUE. HOSPICE CAMP.	January. 1919.		During the first part of the month (see the 19th) the Bn. were engaged in the administration of A and B Hospice Camps receiving troops for demobilization in U.K., and dispatching them in drafts of 100 to the following dispersal stations via Dover and Tilbury. TILBURY. (1) RIPON (VA)(2) HARROWBY (VA)(3) CLIPSTONE (VB VIB) (4) PURFLEET (VA)(5) THETFORD (VA)(6) WATFORD DOVER. (1) KINROSS (IA) DUDDINGSTON (IIA) GEORGETOWN (IB IIB) CHISLEDON (VB, VI) FOVANT (VII) BREEFHEATH (III VA) OSWESTRY (IX XII) CRYSTAL PALACE (XA XIB XC) Working in conjunction with Nos 1 and 2 Camps (not'd Bns) each camp received every fourth day and embarked all men in camp on the morning of the third day where possible. The following are the nos of men dispatched by this new camp till the 19th that, where the 11th R.Sco. Fus. became a purely Reception Division :- Officers. 9 Other Ranks.	
1/1/19			1	774
2/1/19			1	777
3/1/19			2	784

Army Form C. 2118.

WAR DIARY
INTELLIGENCE SUMMARY.
(Erase heading not required.)

Instructions regarding War Diaries and Intelligence Summaries are contained in F. S. Regs., Part II. and the Staff Manual respectively. Title pages will be prepared in manuscript.

Place	Date	Hour	Summary of Events and Information		Remarks and references to Appendices
			Officers	Other Ranks	
DUNKERQUE	6/1/19		1	187	
	7/1/19		7	452	
	7/1/19		19	2,108	
	8/1/19		13	1,516	
	9/1/19		25	1,420	
	9/1/19			591	
	10/1/19			398	
	11/1/19		27	747	
	11/1/19		9	666	
	12/1/19		2	631	
	12/1/19		4	122	
	13/1/19		7	600	
	14/1/19		228	2740	
	15/1/19		26	3740	
	17/1/19		26	700	
	18/1/19		59	1856	

Army Form C. 2118.

WAR DIARY
or
INTELLIGENCE SUMMARY.
(Erase heading not required.)

Instructions regarding War Diaries and Intelligence Summaries are contained in F. S. Regs., Part II. and the Staff Manual respectively. Title pages will be prepared in manuscript.

Place	Date	Hour	Summary of Events and Information	Remarks and references to Appendices
DUNKERQUE	19/1/19		Officers 62 Other Ranks 1987.	
	22/1/19		Hooper Camp became a 'duty' camp – a Reception Division for all those leaving through DUNKIRK for demobilization. On arrival, officers were medically examined and bathed, they were despatched to one of the two Dispatch Divisions (namely Dur. 1, 2; West Riding Regt. B, 4 Camps). A man's camp worked at first on system of receiving by alternate trains, the day's contingent of 5800.	
	28/1/19		Preceded this method in favour of each Camp doing duty in turn for 24 hours, receiving all trains and using accommodation of both camps for that time.	
	30/1/19		3/24 & 2/4 R. Welch Fusiliers arrived to take over B Camp, all R.S.F. personnel remaining to amalgamate in the running of A Camp, as soon as the incoming Battalion was acquainted with its duties. During the month the rate of demobilization gradually reduced, the personnel of the unit and a company of the 2/15th London Regt. was attached to A and B Camp to supplement the staff and enable them to continue to administer the two camps.	

Army Form C. 2118.

WAR DIARY
or
INTELLIGENCE SUMMARY.
(Erase heading not required.)

Instructions regarding War Diaries and Intelligence Summaries are contained in F. S. Regs., Part II. and the Staff Manual respectively. Title pages will be prepared in manuscript.

Place	Date	Hour	Summary of Events and Information	Remarks and references to Appendices
DUNKERQUE	January 1919.		(A) Officers (names) Increase and Decrease of Strength during month.	
	4/1/19		(i) Increase. Capt R.T. Bentley, M.C. 'D' Sq. Border Regt. 3/1/19. from leave.	
	12/1/19		2/Lt A.F. McGoun 'D' " "	
	12/1/19		2/Lt A.J.D. Calvus 'B' " "	
	13/1/19		Capt D.C. Brown 'C' from duty as Town Commandant, Bergues	
	14/1/19		Major A.B. Naylor 'A' from leave	
	17/1/19		Lt. a.m. Kennedy M.C. 'B' "	
	"		2/Lt W.K. Paton 'C' "	
	19/1/19		Lt & Qm. A.T. Cooper 'D' "	
	21/1/19		Major R.E.H. Dicks 'A' "	
	28/1/19		Capt A.J. Bentley, M.C. 'D' "	
			Total. 9	
			(ii) Decrease.	
	11/1/19		Lt R. Strong, M.C. 'A' to Hospital 31/12/18.	
	2/1/19		Lt & Qm. A.T. Cooper 'D' to leave 5/1/19.	
	5/1/19		Major R.E.H. Dicks 'A' to leave 5/1/19.	

Army Form C. 2118.

WAR DIARY
INTELLIGENCE SUMMARY.
(Erase heading not required.)

Instructions regarding War Diaries and Intelligence Summaries are contained in F. S. Regs., Part II. and the Staff Manual respectively. Title pages will be prepared in manuscript.

Place	Date	Hour	Summary of Events and Information	Remarks and references to Appendices
DUNKERQUE	9/1/19		2/Lt. W. Connelly 'A' to U.K. for Demobilization	
	12/1/19		7/Lt. H. J. Graham 'C' do - do -	
	14/1/19		Capt. A. J. Bentley M.C. do leave	
	15/1/19		Capt. D. E. Brown 'D' to Embarkation Camp for demobilization	
	18/1/19		Lt. F. E. Pitt 'A' to U.K. for demobilization	
	21/1/19		Capt. J. Yvellis M.C. 'A' to leave	
	22/1/19		Lt. J. Taylor 'D' to hospital	
	24/1/19		2/Lt. W. Gordon 'B' to leave	
	25/1/19		Lt. J. E. Robson 'B' to U.K. for demobilization	
	26/1/19		2/Lt. Smith P.C.S. 'B' to U.K. for demobilization	
			2/Lt. Harmon W.R. 'C' to U.K. for demobilization	
	27/1/19		Lt. Kennedy W.R. 'C' do - do -	
			Lt. G. B. Henning 'D' to U.K. for Demobilization	
			Lt. C. Gordon Castles 'D' to leave	
	29/1/19		Major W. Pettigrew M.C. 'A' do leave	
	31/1/19		Capt. G. R. N. Macgillicuddy (R.A.M.C.) to leave	
			Total	19

Army Form C. 2118.

WAR DIARY
INTELLIGENCE SUMMARY.
(Erase heading not required.)

Instructions regarding War Diaries and Intelligence Summaries are contained in F. S. Regs., Part II. and the Staff Manual respectively. Title pages will be prepared in manuscript.

Place	Date	Hour	Summary of Events and Information	Remarks and references to Appendices
DUNKERQUE.	Jan. 1919		(B) Alteration to strength during month.	
			(i) Other Ranks (nos).	
			(i) Increase.	
			From Leave	9
			From Hospital or CCS	25
			From Base & Reinforcements	7
			From other units	4
			Total.	42
			(ii) Decrease.	
			To U.K. for Demobilization	189
			To Leave	23
			To Hospital	47
			To Base and other units	8
			Total.	267
	1/2/19.		Net decrease in strength 225	

Alex J. P. Fontaine 2/Lieut
for Intelligence Officer

Army Form C. 2118.

ORDERLY ROOM
11th Bn. Royal Scots Fusiliers
4 MAR 1919
Reg. No. 2/1935/R

WAR DIARY
or
INTELLIGENCE SUMMARY.
(Erase heading not required.)

Instructions regarding War Diaries and Intelligence Summaries are contained in F. S. Regs., Part II. and the Staff Manual respectively. Title pages will be prepared in manuscript.

Place	Date	Hour	Summary of Events and Information	Remarks and references to Appendices
Dunkirk	6/2/19		Battalion re-inforced by 10 Officers & 300 Other Ranks from the 15th 12th Bn. Royal Scots Fusiliers.	
"	6/2/19		No 59299 A/Cpl J May "B" Coy complimented on No 1733 for promptitude, and initiative shown in dealing with an outbreak of fire at Hospice Camp.	
"	10/2/19		Notification received that 59th Division will form part of the Army of Occupation.	
"	14/2/19		No 59721 Pte J McCabe, No 59449 Pte C Tyson, and 53956 Pte J Fletcher awarded the Military Medal.	
"	8/2/19		RSM Jenkins awarded the DSM and presented with ribbon by GOC 59th Division.	

Army Form C. 2118.

WAR DIARY
or
INTELLIGENCE SUMMARY.
(Erase heading not required.)

Instructions regarding War Diaries and Intelligence Summaries are contained in F. S. Regs., Part II. and the Staff Manual respectively. Title pages will be prepared in manuscript.

Place	Date	Hour	Summary of Events and Information	Remarks and references to Appendices
Dunkirk	19/2/19		Extract from London Gazette dated 21st January 1919.	
			"The King has been pleased to approve of the award of the Meritorious Service Medal to the following NCO and NCOs in recognition of valuable service rendered with the Armies in France and Flanders.	
			57939 Co.S.M. Jenkins G. 11th Royal Scots Fusiliers	
			14330 C.Q.M.S. Malley A. 1st Border Regt. attd. 11th R.S.F.	
			4869 Sgt. Berry J. ditto "	
	28/2/19		A & B Camps continued during month to be Reception Camps for all troops arriving for demobilisation. Following are the nos. of Officers and other Ranks passed through these Camps.	
			Officers 1892.	
			O/Rs. 24,525.	

Army Form C. 2118.

WAR DIARY
or
INTELLIGENCE SUMMARY.
(Erase heading not required.)

Instructions regarding War Diaries and Intelligence Summaries are contained in F. S. Regs., Part II. and the Staff Manual respectively. Title pages will be prepared in manuscript.

Place	Date	Hour	Summary of Events and Information	Remarks and references to Appendices
Dunkirk	28/7/14		Dunkirk was used as the Port of Embarkation for the Guards Division returning from Germany to the U.K. The following Battalions passed through their camps during the Month:-	
			2nd Bn Grenadier Guards. 1st Bn Scots Guards	
			3rd " do do 1st " Irish do	
			1st " Coldstream do 2nd " Irish do	
			2nd " do do 1st & 2nd Bns Life Guards M.G. Regt.	
			Royal Horse Guards M.G. Regt.	

Army Form C. 2118.

WAR DIARY
or
INTELLIGENCE SUMMARY.
(Erase heading not required.)

Instructions regarding War Diaries and Intelligence Summaries are contained in F. S. Regs., Part II. and the Staff Manual respectively. Title pages will be prepared in manuscript.

Place	Date	Hour	Summary of Events and Information	Remarks and references to Appendices
DUNKIRK.			Increase and decrease in Strength during month.	
			(A) OFFICERS.	
	February, 2nd.		Lieut. Bolton, to Hospital.	
			2/Lieut. Felgate, to Hospital.	
	Do. 3rd.		Lieut-Colonel. J.N. de la Perrelle, D.S.O. M.C., to Leave.	
	Do. 4th.		Capt. J. Grellis, M.C., from Leave.	
			2/Lieut. W. Goldstein, M.M., to Leave.	
	Do. 6th.		Capt. A.J. Bentley, M.C., to U.K. for Demobilization.	
			Lieut. A.M. Kennedy, M.C. Do.	
			2/Lieut. W.K. Paton, Do.	
	Do. 8th.		2/Lieuts. G.T. King, and A. Heppenstall, Notts and Derbys. Taken on Strength.	
			Lieut-Colonel J.N. de la Perrelle, D.S.O. M.C. from Leave.	
			2/Lieut. W. Goldstein, M.M. from Leave.	
	Do. 9th.		2/Lieut. Felgate, from Hospital.	
			Lieut. R. Strong, M.C., to Leave.	
	Do. 12th.		Major. A.B. Naylor, to U.K., for Demobilization.	

Army Form C. 2118.

WAR DIARY
or
INTELLIGENCE SUMMARY.
(Erase heading not required.)

Instructions regarding War Diaries and Intelligence Summaries are contained in F. S. Regs., Part II. and the Staff Manual respectively. Title pages will be prepared in manuscript.

Place	Date	Hour	Summary of Events and Information	Remarks and references to Appendices
DUNKIRK.	February, 12th.		2/Lieut. J. Sutherland, to U.K. for Demobilization.	
	Do. 13th.		2/Lieut. C. Gordon-Cleather, from Leave.	
			2/Lieut. A.J.D. Porteous, to U.K. for Demobilization.	
			Do. N.C. Donaldson, Do.	
	Do. 15th.		Major. W. Pettigrew, M.C. from Leave.	
	Do. 17th.		2/Lieut. W. Gordon, from Leave.	
			Major. W. Pettigrew, M.C. to U.Kz for Demobilization.	
			Capt. A. Whyte, taken on Strength from 12th. Bn. R.S.F.	
			Lieut. A.W. Inglis, M.C. Do.	
			Lieut. J. M. Smith, M.C. Do.	
			2/Lieut. R.C. Wootton, M.C. Do.	
			Do. A.W. Walker, Do.	
			Capt. T.S. Wyllie, Do.	
			2/Lieut. D. Barr, Do.	
			Do. W.F. Cranston, Do.	
	Do. 20th.		Lieut. J. Rutherford, taken on Strength from 7/8th. K.O.S.B.	

Army Form C. 2118.

WAR DIARY
or
INTELLIGENCE SUMMARY.
(Erase heading not required.)

Instructions regarding War Diaries and Intelligence Summaries are contained in F. S. Regs., Part II. and the Staff Manual respectively. Title pages will be prepared in manuscript.

Place	Date	Hour	Summary of Events and Information	Remarks and references to Appendices
DUNKIRK.	February, 20th.		2/Lieut. A.C.G. Thompson, taken on Strength from 7/8th. K.O.S.B.	
	Do. 21st.		2/Lieut. W. Gordon, to Hospital.	
			2/Lieut. J. McDougall, taken on strength reinforcement.	
			Do. H.N. Jackson, Do.	
			Do. H.D.H.C. Cock, Do.	
			Do. W. Black, Do.	
			Do. W.E.M. Dalziel, Do.	
			Do. J. Fairweather, Do.	
			Do. J.R. McKay, Do.	
			Do. G.B. Robertson, Do.	
			Do. J.H. Scholes, Do.	
			Do. W.P. Fleming, Do.	
			Do. C.G. Jay, Do.	
			Do. D. Campbell, Do.	
	Do. 24th.		Lieut. R. Strong, M.C. from Leave.	
	Do. 25th.		Lieut. R. C. Paterson, to U.K for Demobilization.	
	Do. 27th.		Capt. C. Buckton, 3rd. Lincolns, taken on Strength	

Army Form C. 2118.

WAR DIARY
or
INTELLIGENCE SUMMARY.
(Erase heading not required.)

Instructions regarding War Diaries and Intelligence Summaries are contained in F. S. Regs., Part II. and the Staff Manual respectively. Title pages will be prepared in manuscript.

Place	Date	Hour	Summary of Events and Information	Remarks and references to Appendices
DUNKIRK.			(B). OTHER RANKS.	
			Increase. From Hospital................ 5.	
			" Leave................ 45.	
			" 12th. Bn. R.S.F. (Reinforcec)168.	
			TOTAL. 218.	
			Decrease. To Hospital................ 84.	
			" Leave................ 43.	
			" U.K. for Demobilization..... 221.	
			" Detached................ 3.	
			356.	
			Total decrease in Strength during month.....118. Other Ranks.	

J. van Somerville
Lieut Colonel.
Commdg 11th Bn Royal Scots Fusiliers.

Army Form C. 2118.

WAR DIARY
or
INTELLIGENCE SUMMARY.
(Erase heading not required.)

Instructions regarding War Diaries and Intelligence Summaries are contained in F. S. Regs., Part II. and the Staff Manual respectively. Title pages will be prepared in manuscript.

Place	Date	Hour	Summary of Events and Information	Remarks and references to Appendices
DUNKIRK.	3/5/19	—	Battalion reinforced from 7/8th. Bn. King's Own Scottish Borderers by 2 Officers and 143 Other Ranks.	
Do.	18/5/19.		Lieut-Colonel. J. N. de la Perrelle, D.S.O., M.C. relinquished command of the Battalion on proceeding to Headquarters, Lines of Communication as Chief Disposals Officer and on being promoted Colonel.	
			The following is a copy of Special Order by Lieut-Colonel. J.N. de la Perrelle, on leaving the Battalion:—	
			"Lieut-Colonel. J. N. de la Perrelle, on the occasion of relinquishing the command of the 11th. Bn. Royal Scots Fusiliers and proceeding to another appointment wishes to thank all ranks for their unswavering loyalty and devotion to duty whilst under his command, and expresses the hope that the high standard they have hitherto maintained and which easily gave them the premier position amongst the Battalions of the XI Corps will not only be maintained but improved and enable the 11th. Bn. Royal Scots Fusiliers, to claim that they are the smartest and best disciplined Unit on the Lines of Communication".	
			Major. R.E.H. Dicke assumed command of the Battalion.	
Do.	22/5/19.		Owing to the threatened strikes and Labour Troubles at Home, all Leave and Demobilization was postponed until further notice, Companies were re-organized into Platoons and Sections. Lewis Gun Classes were recommenced.	
Do.	25/5/19.		Restrictions on Leave and Demobilization withdrawn and Camps commenced receiving Troops for demobilization. Training Scheme was held over in abeyance but Lewis Gun Classes with the addition of a class for Signallers still continued their new training.	

A. Bruce Lieut Colonel.
R. Scots Fusiliers

Army Form C. 2118.

WAR DIARY
or
INTELLIGENCE SUMMARY.
(Erase heading not required.)

Instructions regarding War Diaries and Intelligence Summaries are contained in F.S. Regs., Part II. and the Staff Manual respectively. Title pages will be prepared in manuscript.

Place	Date	Hour	Summary of Events and Information	Remarks and references to Appendices
DUNKIRK.			Decease and Increase in strength during the Month of March 1919.	
			(A) O F F I C E R S.	
			(1) Increases. (2) Decreases.	
			Capt. A.B. Paton, M.C. From 7/8th 2/Lieut. C.G. Jay, to Hospital. 3/3/19.	
			K.O.B.Bs. " G.B. Robertson, to Hospital 4/3/19.	
			Lieut. J. Lindsay. Do.	
			Major.C. de W. Armitage.	
			From Abbeyville Area. Capt. G.T. Wright, C.F. To. Leave 14/3/19.	
			Capt. G.T. Wright, C.F. To Lieut-Colonel. J.N. de la Perrelle D.S.O. M.C. to	
			H.Q. L. of C.	
			Lieut. A. Whyte.)	
			" J.McC.Smith.)	
			" A.M. Inglis.) To U.K. for demobilization	
			" S. Wylie.) 18/3/19.	
			2/Lt. D. Barr, M.C.)	
			" E.D.McG. Cook.)	
			2/Lieut. W. Gordon. From Hospital.)	
			" A. Heppinstall. From Leave) Capt. A.B. Paton, M.C. To Leave 19/3/19.	
			18/3/19. 2/Lieut. J. Reid. Transferred to 1/4th. R.S.F. 19/3/19.	
			" A.C.G. Thompson. To D.C. Duty 20/3/19.	
			" J.R. Scholes. To. D.C. Duty 24/3/19.	
			Capt. A.R.N. Macgillycuddy. R.A.M.C. to U.K. for	
			demobilization 24/3/19.	
			Lieut. R. Strong. M.C. to 1/5th. Border Regt. 26/3/19.	
			2/Lieut. J. Fairweather. to U.K. for demobilization	
			Capt. G.T. Wright, C.F. From Leave 28/3/19.	
			30/3/19.	

Army Form C. 2118.

WAR DIARY
or
INTELLIGENCE SUMMARY.
(Erase heading not required.)

DUNKIRK.

Summary of Events and Information

(B) OTHER - RANKS.

(1) Increase.
From Hospital 12
" Reinforcements 17
" Leave 61
                          ———
TOTAL INCREASE.   90.

(2) Decrease.
To Hospital 23
" Demobilization 22
" Leave 77
                          ———
                          122

Decrease during Month 122
Increase   "   90
                          ———
Total Decrease during Month 32. OTHER RANKS.

A. Bruce, Lieut Colonel
Royal Scots Fusiliers

Instructions regarding War Diaries and Intelligence Summaries are contained in F. S. Regs., Part II. and the Staff Manual respectively. Title pages will be prepared in manuscript.

59 Division
178 Infantry Brigade

11 Battalion Royal Scots
Fusiliers

April to June 1919
Missing.

WAR DIARY
or
INTELLIGENCE SUMMARY.
(Erase heading not required.)

Army Form C. 2118.

Place	Date	Hour	Summary of Events and Information	Remarks and references to Appendices
DUNKIRK.	2/7/19.		Lieut. J.K. Murray, M.C. proceeded to H.Q. 178th. Infantry Brigade to learn the duties of Staff Captain. Major. T.H. Oakden, D.S.O. M.C. (1st. Border Regt). proceeded to take over the duties of Commandant, 59th. Divisional School at Beaumaris, CALAIS. Hospice Camp closed down for the receiving of demobilizers night of 30/6/19 - 1/7/19, and Companies commenced Infantry Training. Brig.General R. McDouall, C.M.G., D.S.O., relinquished the command of DUNKIRK BASE, the duties being taken over by Colonel, H.M. Beynon, C.M.G., R.A.	
	3/7/19.			
	6/7/19.		Dunkirk Mounted Sports held on the Aviation Ground, Hospice, St. Pol -sur-Mer 6/7/19.	
	14/7/19.		Dunkirk French Victory March held 14/7/19, the British Army being represented by 4 Officers, 72 Other Ranks, Pipes and Drums of the 11th. Bn. Royal Scots Fusiliers. Inspection Officers General Levi, Commanding, Dunkirk Garrison.	
	19/7/19.		Official Day for the Celebrating of the signing of the Peace Treaty - General Holiday - Dunkirk Garrison Sports held this day. German Firework display held on Brogade Football ground at 2200 hours in the evening. Capt. P. Dale M.C. proceeded to Dunkirk Base Headquarters for duty.	
	21/7/19.		Authority received through Dunkirk Base Routine Orders for the wearing of the British War Medal, 1914-1919.	
	26/7/19		Brig.General T.W. Stansfeld, C.M.G. D.S.O., relinquished the command of the 178th. Infantry Brigade on rproceeding to take over an appointment at home. Brig-General J.H. Pollard, C.B. C.M.G., D.S.O., taking over command.	
	26/7/19.		The following Officer, N.C.O., and man mentioned in Eield Marshal Sir Douglas Haig's despatch dated 16/3/19 :- Lieut (A/Capt.) W. Pettigrew, M.C. 6/7th. Bn. att 11th. Bn. R.S.F. 59648 Cpl. (A/Sgt) C.A. Pedder. No. 265989 Pte. Goss, J.T.	

Army Form C. 2118.

WAR DIARY
or
INTELLIGENCE SUMMARY.

(Erase heading not required.) (2).

Instructions regarding War Diaries and Intelligence Summaries are contained in F. S. Regs., Part II. and the Staff Manual respectively. Title pages will be prepared in manuscript.

Place	Date	Hour	Summary of Events and Information	Remarks and references to Appendices
	JULY, 1919.		OFFICERS MOVEMENTS DURING MONTH.	
			2/Lieut. J. McWhirter. From Leave. 2/7/19.	
			Lieut. J.K. Murray, M.O. To H.Q. 178th. Infantry Brigade. 2/7/19.	
			Major T.H. Oakden, D.S.O. M.C. " 59th. Divisional School as Commandant. 2/7/19.	
			2/Lieut. F. Stothart, " Hospital 7/7/19.	
			2/Lieut. A. Heppinstall,(M.&.D) From Leave 10/7/19.	
			Lieut. W. Smellie, M.C. To Leave 13/7/19.	
			2/Lieut. T.M. Felgate (Essex) " 18/7/19.	
			2/Lieut. R. Hamilton, (R.S.F.) From 1/4th. R.S.F. 19/7/19z	
			Lieut. P. Dale, M.C. To Dunkirk Base H.Q. 19/7/19.	
			Capt. G.T. Wright, C.F. " Leave 22/7/19.	
			2/Lieut. W. Goldstein (S.Staffs) " (VERQUIN) 23/7/19.	
			2/Lieut. R. Martin. " " 25/7/19.	
			Capt. M. Gilmour. " " 27/7/19.	
			INCREASES AND DECREASE IN STRENGTH DURING MONTH.	
			(A). OFFICERS.	
			Total Decrease during month .... 4.	
			(B) OTHER RANKS.	
			(See Page 3).	

Army Form C. 2118.

WAR DIARY
or
INTELLIGENCE SUMMARY.
(Erase heading not required.)

Place	Date	Hour	Summary of Events and Information	Remarks and references to Appendices
DUNKIRK.			"B" OTHER RANKS.	
			INCREASE.	
			From G.B.D. 9	
			" Leave 59	
			" Hospital 10	
			" Other Causes 3	
			81	
			Decrease 9	
			690	
			DECREASE.	
			To Demobilisation............. 2	
			Hospital.................... 20	
			Leave 64	
			Other Causes 4	
			90	
			A.Bruce	
			Lieut-Colonel,	
			Commanding, 11th. Bn. Royal Scots Fusiliers.	

www.ingramcontent.com/pod-product-compliance
Lightning Source LLC
Chambersburg PA
CBHW081435160426
43193CB00013B/2289